Praise for Being Numerous

"I am always thrilled to read work by Natasha Lennard. Her combination of theory and hard reporting is as rare as it is essential. Questions about liberalism and anti-fascism that dominate our political moment are tackled here with theoretical sophistication, serious reporting, and an inimitable style." —Sarah Leonard, coeditor of *The Future We Want: Radical Ideas for the New Century*

"In meditations on riots and surveillance, sex radicalism and First Amendment controversies, Lennard—who moved to the United States from London a decade ago and is now one of the most astute thinkers to emerge from the Occupy movement—offers a crystalline vision of how fascism can be fought without reliance on the state and why it must be" —*The Nation*

"Lennard doesn't shy away from telling us the uncomfortable truth: Within each of us, she says, there lies a love of power, authority, and social hierarchy we must work to undo every day to live a non-fascist life." —*Vice*

"Natasha Lennard views politics through the lens of theory, and writes theory with passion and fire—her essays on suicide, violence, sex and antifascism are the work of a dazzling intellect grappling with the most pressing issues of our time." —Molly Crabapple, author of *Drawing Blood*

"This book is a must read for those interested in elegant and clever writing on the urgent political and social issues of our day. Natasha Lennard offers sharp perspectives on the stale and complacent polarization of left and right. And there is a power and freshness here: amidst the glimpses of the personal—while often couched in erudite philosophical discourse—she reveals herself to be a woman and thinker of substance." —Razia Iqbal, journalist at BBC News

Being Numerous

Essays on Non-Fascist Life

Natasha Lennard

VERSO

London • New York

This paperback edition published by Verso 2021
First published by Verso 2019
© Natasha Lennard 2019, 2021

This book draws on essays that have appeared in
The Evergreen Review, *Real Life*, *Vice*, *Esquire*, *The Nation*,
Salon, *Logic*, *Fusion*, and *The New Inquiry*.

1 3 5 7 9 10 8 6 4 2

Verso
UK: 6 Meard Street, London W1F 0EG
US: 20 Jay Street, Suite 1010, Brooklyn, NY 11201
versobooks.com

Verso is the imprint of New Left Books

ISBN-13: 978-1-78873-460-8
ISBN-13: 978-1-78873-462-2 (US EBK)
ISBN-13: 978-1-78873-461-5 (UK EBK)

British Library Cataloguing in Publication Data
A catalogue record for this book is available from the British Library

The Library of Congress Has Cataloged the Hardback Edition As Follows:
Names: Lennard, Natasha, author.
Title: Being numerous : essays on non-fascist life / Natasha Lennard
Description: London ; New York : Verso, 2019. | Includes index. | Summary:
"An urgent challenge to the prevailing moral order from one of the freshest,
most compelling voices in radical politics today."--
Provided by publisher.
Identifiers: LCCN 2019286300 (print) | ISBN
9781786634818 (hardback) | ISBN 9781788734622 (ebook)
Subjects: LCSH: Conservatism--United States--History--21st century. |
Political culture--United States--21st century. | United States--Politics and
government--2017.
Classification: LCC E912 .L46 2019
DDC 973.933092--dc23
LC record available at https://lccn.loc.gov/2019286300

Typeset in Sabon by MJ & N Gavan, Truro, Cornwall
Printed in the UK by CPI Group

For my mother, Sindy, and my person, Lukas.

Having only the force
Of days

Most simple
Most difficult
—George Oppen, 1968

Contents

Introduction

I was attending a memorial in late 2016. The previous night, an old friend had been thrown from a car as it flipped, swerving to avoid a deer carcass on a Wisconsin highway. He had been en route to join the protests against the Dakota Access Pipeline at Standing Rock in North Dakota.

I met Clark in 2010, about a year after I'd moved to New York from London for graduate school. We were part of a book club called "the anti-state communist reading group," or something to that dramatic effect. The friendships forged there became the foundation of an anarchist-leaning cadre, which helped fuel Occupy Wall Street with radical, sometimes blustery, leftist energy. Rake thin, beanstalk tall, mustachioed and grinning, Clark was a mischievous and above-all generous activist. We were thick as thieves for some years, but drifted apart in the time before his death. No animosity—we chose different projects, different spaces; far-left organizing in New York cleaved along ideological and personal lines. But the presence of Clark's absence, or his absent presence, was reason enough for a splintered scene to come together again that winter night in a community bookshop in Queens.

It was the evening of November 8, 2016. We weren't looking at our phones, and I didn't see the infographic maps of the United States turning red. Before midnight Eastern time, Donald Trump would take Indiana, Kentucky, swing state Ohio, and battleground Florida. We drank to our friend and lit candles, oblivious.

"We are pressed, pressed on each other / We will be told at once / Of anything that happens." So wrote poet George Oppen in his 1968 work *Of Being Numerous,* and it's truer today, thanks to technocapital, than when the poem was written. But that night, on the eve of the Trump era, pressing together for those few hours, we were not told at once of the results rolling in.

Four years later, I learned of Trump's electoral defeat through the sound of pots and pans banging, horns blaring, and uproarious cheers erupting from my block in Crown Heights, Brooklyn. The area was one of the hardest hit when Covid-19 first ravaged New York City in early spring. On an unusually warm November Saturday, Trump lost, and a weekend of music followed—sounds not of bold rebellion, like those that had reverberated through the streets in early summer, but of short-lived relief.

More lines from that same Oppen poem come to mind: "It is the air of atrocity, / An event as ordinary / As a President / A plume of smoke, visible at a distance / In which people burn."

Before he died, Clark wrote a political call of sorts in a scribbled note: "Live how we want to. Account for real needs and desires whilst making a million and one sacrifices. Do anything for each other ... Fight so hard that we don't feel as if we're going to explode all the time, make that the great American pastime again." His best friend read out those words at the memorial. An invocation toward non-fascist life, written before the shuddering fact of a President Trump.

Now, in the midst of a death-dealing pandemic, in the wake of a relieving yet depressing presidential election, with the promise of ongoing, powerful uprisings and the grim assurance of future fascist violences, new urgency attends old questions of how we press and are pressed upon each other— of the meaning of being numerous.

Many of us have considered anew at which junctions, through which quotidian flows, our breaths and spits mingle and our individual bodies reveal their porousness. The determinations of racial capitalism have left little ambiguity as to who gets forced to work in perilous proximity, and left without care, to die. Yet the Black-led rebellions of summer 2020 were an unparalleled lesson in how we must press together with ferocity against the white supremacist necropolitics of the now. The uprisings—for Black life and liberation—clarified the scope and shape of contemporary American fascism and anti-fascism in a way that no preceding debates around Trump ever could.

Following the 2016 election, people took to the streets in great numbers across the country; the New York crowds I joined were diverse and young. The chant went up, "No Trump! No KKK! No fascist USA!"; I wondered then if the youngest among us, or those newest to protest, knew that this slogan was a riff on an old favorite, "No cops! No KKK! No fascist USA!" If they did not then, they may now, thanks to the necessary rebellions of 2020—which were larger and more resilient than any protest with Trump as its singular focus had ever been.

I began with Trump's election victory and loss not because this collection is strictly organized around his presidency. A number of the essays herein were first written some years before Trump's ascendance, others after his rise, and the most recent after his electoral defeat. It is unavoidable, though, that his tenure haunts every piece, compiled as they are in this moment of emboldened racist fascism. I recall the 2016 election night here—*my* election night, shaped as it was by a most different type of loss and haunting—to invoke the idea of accidents. In a sense, accidents are the proper subject of this book.

I don't mean happenstances, or missteps—too many liberal commentators misframe our current political moment as a baffling mistake, as history taking some wrong turn. I mean "accident" as it was framed by late theorist and urbanist Paul Virilio: the accident as that which is contained within, and brought into the world by, the inventions of progress—or what gets hailed as progress—itself.

"When you invent the ship, you also invent the shipwreck; when you invent the plane you also invent the plane crash; and when you invent electricity, you invent electrocution," he wrote. "Every technology carries its own negativity, which is invented at the same time as technical progress." Invent the car, invent the car crash. Invent nuclear power, invent the H-bomb. Invent networked online communications, invent totalized, mutually enforced surveillance. Invent new mechanisms by which to extract resources from parts of the world previously untouched by human industry, and introduce new deadly pandemics to human populations. The accident is not the inevitability—the advent of the car did not, of course, determine any given car crash—but it brought to life the possibility of such things, to which we are all too often blinded by the propaganda of progress as some smooth, unidirectional passage. Accidents happen; technical progress determines what kind of accidents can exist.

Virilio applied the concept of the accident to technological advancement and its logic of acceleration. But the idea is useful broadly, when looking at the operations through which society, selves and power are produced and organized. For example, if the current growth of fascism is an accident, in a sense cribbed from Virilio, it is not because it is a diversion, antithetical to liberal capitalism. The accident was baked into the context.

What follows in this collection, written and updated over the last six years of my career as a columnist, journalist and essayist, is a series of pieces, each of which takes aim at how liberal, capitalist ideology—and its sometimes-fanatical commitment to Enlightenment promises—fails to address its own potential accidents and limitations. Any muted contentment about a new US president must be all the more tempered through considerations of the accidents, in Virilio's use of the term, inherent to the Biden administration's so-called centrism.

Liberal centrism is conservative. Many progressive victories claimed by its adherents were built on the back, at least in part, of decades of radical struggle. Liberal centrists cling to a paradoxical progress of conservation; its adherents seem to long for the halcyon delusions of pre–November 8, 2016, and the hope that the new president will deliver us there. Under Trump, the chants went up: "America was always great" (it was never); "Not my president!" (he was). The *New York Times* proclaimed, "Truth can't be manufactured" (it can, it is, and the *Times* should know); the *Washington Post* developed a new tagline reading "Democracy dies in darkness," (it dies in broad daylight, too). Unwilling to reckon with their accidents, which are not mistakes, centrist ideologues fail to offer weapons, let alone a sturdy shield, against the fascism of the state, the white supremacist constellations it encourages, and the micro-fascisms that permeate daily life and habit. This book is a call for better weapons and an expansive understanding of the battlefield, where oppressive systems hold territory in ever more brutal ways.

Jean-Paul Sartre described, in his 1937 novel *Nausea*, how "things happen one way and we tell about them in the opposite sense." His protagonist reflects: "You seem to start at the beginning. And in reality you have started at the end. It was there, invisible and present, it is the one which gives to words the pomp and value of a beginning." I didn't begin any of the following essays with the intention, or even the idea, of compiling them. That's the nature of recounting—starting at the end, seeing patterns emerge, a thread of consistent argument and politics, in work I have written as discrete pieces over the years on themes ranging from riots, racial capitalism, political violence and the limits of a rights discourse, to ghosts (which are not metaphors), corpses, sex, suicide, the state and the self. That they come together is a happy accident, which is no coincidence at all.

December 2020

We, Anti-Fascists

Between spells of January drizzle, in the midst of scattered street protests, on a particularly bad afternoon in Washington, DC, Richard Spencer got punched in the face.

That morning, Donald Trump commenced his term as president with rageful, nationalistic oration. Nearby, police penned in and mass-arrested over 200 inauguration counter-protesters. The demonstrators, participants in an "anti-fascist, anti-capitalist bloc"—in which I had also marched—would go on to face a repressive array of bogus felony charges and potential decades in prison. By the afternoon of January 20, protests were dispersed, gloating frat boys in red "Make America Great Again" hats ambled through DC's dreary avenues, and Donald Trump was president.

Any silver lining that day was going to be thin. But there it was, gleaming: a sublime right hook to Richard Spencer's face.

I didn't see it in person, but on a YouTube clip, which during the coming weeks would be viewed well over 3 million times.

Spencer, a neo-Nazi who claims America belongs to white men, was in the middle of telling an Australian TV crew that he was not a neo-Nazi, while pointing to the white nation-alist mascot, Pepe the Frog, on his lapel pin. A black-clad figure, face covered (the unofficial uniform of our march that morning) jumps into frame, deus ex machina, with a flying punch to Spencer's left jaw. The alt-right poster boy stumbles away, and his anonymous attacker bounds out of sight.

Within hours it was a meme, set to backing tracks from Springsteen, New Order, Beyoncé and dozens more. A thing of kinetic beauty, the punch was made for an anthem's beat; the punch was made for sharing.

I had thought we could all agree: a prominent neo-Nazi was punched in the face; it was a good thing.

I had miscalculated "we."

In the weeks and months prior to Trump's inauguration, an outpouring of media commentary was dedicated to determining whether the soon-to-be president was or was not a fascist, and whether we were or were not on the verge of living under a fascist regime. Characteristics like selective populism, nationalism, racism, traditionalism, the deployment of Newspeak and a disregard for reasoned debate were rightly noted as fascist tendencies, if not sufficient for some to call the Trump phenomenon a fascist one.

These articles spoke to a genuine panic that the arc of history had been bent in the wrong direction, twisting back on itself toward early twentieth-century Europe. They were steeped in modernity's progress myth, conveniently forgetting that fascism has, in fact, always been continuous with modernity. Whether or not the commentators concluded that Trump was an *actual* fascist, they all agreed that fascism was to be understood as The Worst. This glut of commentary treated fascism as something that takes shape only in the context of a historically constituted regime—the problem of fascism was real, but located only in the threat of its possible return: *Will Donald Trump bring fascism to America?*

It was as if decades of theorizing fascism—as an ideology, or a tendency, a practice, something that never quite disappeared —had been erased overnight and all that mattered in the media frenzy was delineating Trump's similarities and differences to Hitler or Mussolini.

I didn't consider at the time that most of the commentators weighing in on Trump's fascism (or lack thereof) presumed their position to be anti-fascist enough. Every argument was premised on the post–World War II a priori that fascism is an evil to which we are opposed: a departure from or aberration of the sociopolitical status quo, something outside of ourselves. It's perhaps no accident that a liberal commentariat would focus on this sort of state fascism—one that reductive histories pretend was conquered by liberal democracy, rather than crumbled in protracted war. But there's nothing so easy, nor so empty, as opposition to a fascism that is framed as an unparalleled historical horror that *could* return.

I took in good faith these professed concerns about the Trumpian specter of fascism, and I believed in turn that we would see a broad liberal-to-left acceptance of vigorous anti-fascist action. And so, I advocated, and continue to advocate, for a particular response to perceived fascism, one that has enjoyed successes throughout the twentieth and early twenty-first centuries. I'm talking about the anti-fascism abbreviated as "Antifa"—a militant, no-tolerance approach to far-right, racist nationalism, the sort that, while it is not new, has become newly empowered and utterable. As such, I am talking about that messy, instable, ever-oversimplified category: violence. Or, as I see it, counterviolence. I delighted, publicly, in Richard Spencer getting punched.

Antifa is not a group, nor a movement, nor even an identity. To state one's political position as anti-fascist after 1945 is close to empty and, I will argue, in a certain sense necessarily false. But as a practice taken up by the pan–far left (socialist and anarchist alike), Antifa is an illiberal intervention that in resisting fascism does not rely on the state, the justice system or any liberal institution. It finds organization online, in the streets, on campuses—wherever fascism is to be found.

Having spent much of my writing career arguing against the old canard of violence versus nonviolence, I did not think liberal aversions to the idea of political violence would suddenly vanish. But I thought, with fear of fascism in the air and a clamor for some unified resistance, that we could at least agree that it was okay, if not good, to punch a neo-Nazi. How wrong I was.

The gleeful social media circulation of the Spencer punch video was met with censure from the same liberal media microcosms that had spent the previous weeks nail-biting about fascism. Even the most simply Antifa act—a silencing, anti-Nazi punch—would not find broad support in the so-called resistance.

A year into the Trump presidency, I felt like I'd fallen through the looking glass. The apparent panic about the rise of fascism had been overtaken by paranoiac fear and condemnation of the rise of anti-fascism.

I had thought that Charlottesville would take on the valence of historic Event—the sort about which we speak of "before" and "after"; a turning point. A neo-Nazi plowed his Dodge Charger into a crowd of anti-fascist counterprotesters, killing one and injuring many. A young Black man was viciously beaten by racists with metal poles in a parking lot by a police station. White supremacists marched, Klan-like, with burning torches and Nazi salutes around a Confederate statue of General Robert E. Lee while chanting, "Jews will not replace us!"—a gruesome pastiche of nineteenth-century American and twentieth-century European race hate, never vanquished but newly Trump-emboldened. The day after the rally, the president blamed "many sides." Some days later, like a pantomime villain at another campaign-less campaign rally in Phoenix, he let out an ominous roar: "Anteefa!"

In Charlottesville, the already-flimsy veil of plausible deniability about the racist fascism of the so-called alt-right had been ripped away. Faced with the spectacle of Charlottesville, liberal commentators who had written baseless screeds comparing the threat of far-left anti-fascists to that of white nationalism would surely think twice about such a false equivalency.

Upon hearing the "two sides" argument from the puckered, impossible mouth of the president, I was sure the mainstream narrative equating far-left and far-right violence would shift. Instead, it doubled down. In the month that followed the intolerable events in Charlottesville, America's six top broadsheet newspapers ran twenty-eight opinion pieces condemning anti-fascist action, but only twenty-seven condemning neo-Nazis, white supremacists and Trump's failure to disavow them.

Meanwhile, magazines and news outlets—only a year ago lousy with warnings against the "normalization" of hate—have published a string of profiles platforming white supremacists and neo-Nazis as if they were now an accepted part of the social fabric (thus interpellating them as such). The "polite" Midwestern Hitler fan with a Twin Peaks tattoo whose manners "would please anyone's mother." The "dapper" white nationalist. The description of right extremist rallies drenched in dog whistle and foghorn neo-Nazi symbolism as mere "pro-Trump" gatherings—or worse, as "free speech" rallies.

What changed? In truth, nothing. We are observing a phenomenon that Martin Luther King Jr. noted well in his 1963 "Letter from a Birmingham Jail." We are dealing with "the white moderate, who is more devoted to 'order' than to justice; who prefers a negative peace which is the absence of tension to a positive peace which is the presence of justice; who constantly says: 'I agree with you in the goal you seek, but I cannot agree with your methods of direct action.'" There is no shortage of irony in the invocation of MLK by today's white moderates in order to decry Antifa tactics as violent; in fact, I believe (if one can so speculate) that these same commentators would have been critical of his radical nonviolence, predicated as it was on the provocation of violent spectacle. It is a great liberal tradition to stand on the wrong side of history until that history is comfortably in the past.

~

We're seeing a liberal aversion to violence, but it is one that fails to locate violence in the right places.

Any discussion about violence and Antifa must note that since 1990, there have been 450 deaths caused by white supremacist violence in the United States, compared to only one believed to be related to far-left activity. While property damage, minor clashes and a few neo-Nazi black eyes drew cries of leftist extremism in the last year, an active white supremacist traveled to New York with the precise aim of murdering Black men. He succeeded in stabbing and killing a homeless man. In Portland, Oregon, another white supremacist killed two men who were standing up for two Muslim women on a train. Outside a talk by right-wing commentator Milo Yiannopoulos in Seattle, one of his fans, wearing a "Make America Great Again" cap, shot and wounded an anti-fascist counterprotester in the stomach. To name but a few examples. In the ten days that followed Trump's election alone, the Southern Poverty Law Center reported 900 separate incidents of bias and violence against immigrants, Latinos, African Americans, women, LGBTQ people, Muslims and Jews.

Centrist liberals criticize Antifa activists for responding with counterviolence, urging instead that we follow Michelle Obama's gracious direction: "When they go low, we go high." Insisting on the importance of debate with fascists, they decry violent or confrontational intervention.

Some see tactical and moral value in allowing the likes of Richard Spencer to speak publicly and rally, believing that the fallacies of their hateful views are best made visible and therefore subject to debate and reason. The idea, then, is that the best way to defeat hate speech, such as vile arguments for race realism, would be to listen to it and thus allow its internal contradictions and idiocy to thwart itself.

This is wishful thinking, proven false by the actual state of things—tantamount to telling a patient with a pus-seeping wound that sunlight is the best disinfectant. The alt-right

might be a fumbling fractured mess, and the white supremacists in the White House make their buffoonery clear. But
support for racist ideology and its mainstream normalization
are not dwindling by virtue of this—quite the opposite. This
is not a fringe group whose unreasoned racism, if articulated
and forcefully debated, will lose traction and self-implode.

In a recent video that earned a lot of liberal praise, *Guardian*
journalist Gary Younge interviewed Richard Spencer. Younge
recounted the encounter as follows: "In the course of our
exchange he claims that Africans contributed nothing to civi-
lisation (they started it), that Africans benefited from white
supremacy (they didn't) and that, since I'm Black I cannot be
British (I am)." His retelling is accurate, and Spencer's facade
equally paper thin, but this did nothing to impede Spencer's
bluster. In the video, a flustered Younge tells Spencer, "You're
really proud of your racism, aren't you … you're talking
nonsense." Spencer, unmoved, continues, "You'll never be an
Englishman." A racist for whom the tenets of white supremacy
are foundational will not be swayed by Younge's correctness.
This was neither interlocution, nor a particularly revelatory
exposure of Spencer's well-publicized views; this was the
incommensurability of a white supremacist Weltanschauung
with one of tolerance.

Liberal appeals to Truth will not break through to a fascist
epistemology of power and domination—these are Spencer
and his ilk's first principles. And it is this aspect of fascism that
needs to be grasped to understand the necessity of Antifa's
confrontational tactics.

There is no one uniting ideology between those—across history
and geography—who see Antifa practices as the best means to
combat certain fascist iterations. I say "certain" because neo-
Nazi and white supremacist groups, public figures, and (in our
case) presidents are not the sum total of fascism. Even their
total obliteration would not rid us of fascism.

Rather, each is simply a dangerous locus of what I want to call "fascistic habit"—formed of fascistic desire to dominate, oppress and obliterate the nameable "other." (I don't use the word "habit" lightly; I mean no less than the modes by which we live). Their fascism is not a perversion of our society's business as usual, but an outgrowth. I won't talk of "neo-fascism" any more than I will talk of "neo-Antifa"; for fascism never disappeared but simply reiterates, sometimes with greater force. Antifa, as I see it, is one aspect of a broader abolitionist project, which would see all racist policing, prisons and oppressive hierarchies abolished. As German Social Democrat and playwright Bertolt Brecht wrote in 1935, "How can anyone tell the truth about Fascism, unless he is willing to speak out against capitalism, which brings it forth?"

Also writing in Germany during the early 1930s, Freudian acolyte Wilhelm Reich wrestled with the operations by which a society *chooses* a fascist, authoritarian system. Rejecting narratives in which ignorant masses are duped or led into supporting a system they do not in fact want, he instead insisted that if we are to explain the rise of fascism, we must account for the fact that people, en masse, choose and desire fascism, and that we must understand their desire as genuine. Reich's diagnosis—that the fascist subject is the product of societally enforced sexual repression, and can be thus treated with psychoanalysis—is biologically essentialist, overly general and totally out of date. Nevertheless, his reckoning with fascistic desire is something sorely lacking in this moment of Trump-emboldened fascism and the battle against it.

Certain lines from Reich's *The Mass Psychology of Fascism* (1933) get regurgitated more than others in moments like this—moments in which a media cottage industry seems dedicated to defining fascism in order to prove that we are, or are not, faced with it. "Fascist mentality is the mentality of the subjugated 'little man' who craves authority and rebels against it at the same time"—that's a popular one, and apt.

So is the reflection that it is "not by accident that all fascist dictators stem from the milieu of the little reactionary man." However, I'm more interested in some of his less-cited observations, in particular those that describe the *everyday* forms of fascism: that "there is today not a single individual who does not have the elements of fascist feeling and thinking in his structure"; and that "one cannot make the Fascist harmless if, according to the politics of the day, one looks for him only in the German or Italian, or the American or the Chinese; if one does not look for him in oneself; if one does not know the social institutions which hatch him every day."

Reich's insight is not restricted to Germany during Hitler's rise. The problem of everyday fascisms—micro-fascisms with and by which we live—is real and complicates the fascist/anti-fascist dichotomy; indeed, there is a certain impossibility to "anti-fascist" as an identity. Among the twentieth-century thinkers who have built on Reich's idea of a perverted desire for fascism, perhaps most notable are the French philosopher Gilles Deleuze and psychoanalyst Félix Guatarri. They wrote that it is "too easy to be anti-fascist on the molar level, and not even see the fascist inside of you." In his famed introduction to their 1972 text *Anti-Oedipus*, theorist Michel Foucault noted, "The fascism in us all, in our heads and in our everyday behaviour, the fascism that causes us to love power, to desire the very thing that dominates and exploits us."

So if in this sense we are all somehow possessed of fascism, how can we speak of anti-fascism, and how can we name and delineate the fascists of our political targeting? It is precisely through the recognition of fascism as a developed tendency. The fascism Deleuze and Guattari are talking about is not some innate disease or pathology that we can't shake, but rather a perversion of desire produced through forms of life under capitalism and modernity: practices of authoritarianism and domination and exploitation that form us, such that we can't just "decide" our way out of them. But not everyone becomes a neo-Nazi; only a few people seek the white supremacy that grimly organizes society as it stands. This, too, takes fascist practice, fascist habit; a nurturance and constant reaffirmation of that fascistic desire to oppress and live in an oppressive world. And, to be sure, the world provides that pernicious affirmation: Donald Trump is president, after all.

How to break a habit? Thought, therapy, or reasoning may sometimes prove useful. Sometimes. There are rare stories of neo-Nazis who left the movement that way. On the other hand, the introduction of serious consequences, if not breaking the habit entirely, may redirect it such that its practices cannot be continued, fed or maintained. When "serious consequences" are taken to mean brushes with criminal justice and the carceral system, that simply introduces state-sanctioned fascistic practices into the mix (not to mention the unlikelihood of the US criminal justice system treating white supremacy as an enemy). This is the importance of anti-fascism also as practice and habit: if desire for fascism is not something that happens out of reason, then we cannot break it with reason. So our interventions must instead make the entertainment and maintenance of fascist living intolerable. The desire for fascism will not be thus undone: it is by its nature self-destructive. But at least the spaces for it to be nurtured and further normalized will be withdrawn.

And what of the fascisms in each of us who would be anti-fascist? "Kill the cop inside your head!" goes the anarchist dictum. As philosopher John Protevi noted in his 2000 essay, following Deleuze and Guatarri, "A thousand independent and self-appointed policemen do not make a Gestapo, though they may be a necessary condition for one." How do we remove ourselves as participants in such a condition? Easier said than done. We cannot simply be anti-fascist; we must also practice and make better habits, forms of life. Rather than as a noun or adjective, *anti-fascist* as a gerund verb: a constant effort of *anti-fascisting* against the fascisms that even we ourselves uphold. Working to create nonhierarchical ways of living, working to undo our own privileges and desires for power. The individualized and detached Self, the over-codings of family-unit normativity, the authoritarian tendency of careerism—all of them paranoiac sites of micro-fascism in need of anti-fascist care. Again, easier said than done. But better than a faulty approach to anti-fascism that frames it as some pure position, when it is anything but. We act against fascists in the knowledge we need to act against ourselves, too. The strategy is always to create consequences for living a fascist life and seek anti-fascist departures.

But if we continue to reject outright such anti-fascist consequences for explicit neo-Nazis, the effort, which has no obvious end, will be stymied from the outset.

Fascism is un-bannable. Last summer I was in Berlin when German neo-Nazis planned an authorized march in the western reaches of the city. "Do you know anything about this march in Spandau on Saturday?" an American friend who'd recently moved to Berlin emailed to ask. "I thought neo-Nazi demonstrations weren't even allowed here?"

They aren't, and they are. In statutes that made German speech no less free than ours, the display or reproduction of Hitler-era symbols like the swastika or the Nazi-salute is banned; the legal concept of Volksverhetzung—literally "incitement of the masses," actually "incitement of hatred"—criminalizes Holocaust denial and an array of hate speech. But on August 17, 2017, over 500 neo-Nazis in their own makeshift uniforms of white T-shirts and khakis attempted to march to mark the anniversary of the death of high-ranking Nazi official Rudolf Hess. Five days after Charlottesville I went to the counterprotest with my partner—a born and raised Berliner—a few friends, and a hope to see the rally disrupted, but no experience with or close connections to Berlin Antifa.

Before they could amass, the Nazis—great lunking gobs of pink-white flesh and bile in white cotton—passed through police tents to be checked for weapons and contraband symbols. Some emerged with black tape over verboten tattoos. They stood in phalanx formation, some waving the black, white and red flag of the German Empire, the early Weimar Republic and the Nazi regime until 1935. A particular tranche of the German extremist right: not the Islamophobic thugs of Pegida (Patriotic Europeans Against the Islamisation of the Occident), or the polished Alternative for Deutschland (founded by conservative elites in 2013, and by 2017 the third-largest political party in Germany), but traditional Third Reich–nostalgic neo-Nazis marching in Berlin. Rows and rows of cops in Robocop riot gear protected them as they prepared to march. (Police protect Nazi marches in America with equal vigor; by contrast, one Black Lives Matter march I attended was shut down even before it could leave New York's Union Square.)

We few hundred counterprotesters couldn't get close, so we instead sat in the street, blocking the march route to the site of the prison where Hess was once held. The police moved in, dragging the seated crowd out of the street one by one, with visible sadism. Fingers pressed on eye sockets; faces pushed against gravel; young, small bodies dragged by the neck. As more and more of us sat, the police gave up. So we remained there, and the Nazis remained there. Eventually they turned around, briefly marched in the wrong direction, and dispersed. None of my Jewish family died in the Holocaust; they left Russia for England in the 1890s. I'm white, endowed with that privilege, and I never felt Jewish until I was in Berlin, where the little *Stolpersteine* (stumbling stones) of brass, bearing the names and life dates of Jewish victims of the Nazis dot the pavement in front of where they had lived or worked. You notice them, and then you don't. They don't trip you up. I've never felt more Jewish than I did when standing feet away from red-faced Nazis paying homage to Rudolf Hess. I also felt sick. They deserve a fiercer consequence than a blocked street and a taped-up swastika tattoo. Last year, Germany saw nearly 22,000 attacks motivated by far-right sentiment, a 42 percent increase from 2015. This is what a state ban on neo-Nazis looks like.

After I left Berlin, I visited my elderly grandfather in southern Spain. He's a British expat with a vast repertoire of embellished anecdotes, a purpling tan and the occasional reactionary bent. Once at lunch, I asked him, "Do you think it's okay to punch neo-Nazis?"

I asked him, in particular, because I was seeking a certain response, from a certain generation, at a certain distance. I wanted an incredulous "yes" and a confused expression, as if I'd asked whether fire burns or if he'd like another drink. He's the sort of man who sees the world as if moral facts were just *there*, as obvious and immovable as mountains. While I recognized this is not the constant ethical navigation of anti-fascisting we need, I nevertheless wanted my grandfather—whose politics are not my own—to place neo-Nazi-punching in his blunt taxonomy of Right and Wrong. I wanted to beg my own question.

He replied without pause, as I had hoped: "Who could have a problem with that?" He told me that his father, my great-grandfather, had joined the 43 Group—the network of Jewish ex-servicemen and their allies who, in the streets of postwar England, fought bloody battles against supporters of Oswald Mosley, the former leader of the British Union of Fascists (BUF). My great-grandfather's involvement in the group is an unverified note of family folklore, but one I choose to maintain. It's feasible: he was a Jewish Londoner who served in the British Army, and at its height around 1,000 people were involved in 43 Group activity. But Grandpa gave no further details; we finished lunch and he retired from the veranda sun to sleep. I presume he felt the comment about his father's involvement bore a self-contained sufficiency—as if the 43 Group were not merely a historic point of reference, but a moral fact, such that the invocation of the name alone was enough to assert that this was a Good.

The 43 Group was an anti-fascist organization that deployed violence as its primary tactic. Its founding members had returned from the war with the presumption that their work fighting fascism had ended with Hitler's downfall. It seemed unthinkable that the once-flourishing prewar fascist movement, led by the aristocratic, anti-Semitic politician Mosley, could be revived. What does it mean to reckon with the desire for fascism at the very moment the death spectacle of the camps could not be unseen by the world? But the ex-servicemen who founded the 43 Group returned from the war to find Mosley and his fascists regrouping, rallying and organizing in growing numbers. They speechified about the threat of an "alien menace." Synagogues and Jewish cemeteries in East London were vandalized. "They didn't burn enough of them in Belsen"—so went the chant during fascist mobilizations, referencing the infamous Nazi concentration camp.

In response, the anti-fascists of the 43 Group made it their business not only to identify and surveil, but to physically confront, disrupt and shut down postwar fascist organizing in London and across Britain. "We're not here to kill. We're here to maim," they would say—and indeed, they wielded knives, knuckledusters and crowbars. The group disrupted over 2,000 meetings over five active years and is widely credited for its success neutralizing postwar Britain's fascist movement. "We defended the community by making it impossible for the fascists to terrorize us," one member, Jules Konopinski, told the *Guardian* in 2009. The group's militancy drew some contemporary censure from parts of the British Jewish establishment, but for the most part its place in history is either overlooked or lauded by historians, Holocaust memorial institutions and anti-racist groups. Famed hairdresser Vidal Sassoon was an active fighter among the group, and when he died in 2012, mainstream media obituaries described him as an "anti-fascist warrior" who was "fighting back against fascist oppression."

Fast-forward to January 2017, when I was publicly chastised for celebrating one artful Antifa punch delivered to Richard Spencer's face, caught on meme-ready video. It is a classic instance of historical NIMBYism—taken up by liberals and conservatives alike—in which it is only in the past, or in other countries, that violent militancy against white supremacy constitutes legitimate resistance. This logic is premised on the belief (even the tacit one) that while dissent, militancy and violence is fine *there* and was fine *then*, our current context is not so bad. We imprison today's protesters and canonize yesterday's insurrectionists.

We must undo this NIMBYism and reckon with the violence of the here and now. Even if anti-fascists couldn't get close enough for physical confrontation on the day the neo-Nazis marched in Berlin, it was nevertheless a violent event, even before the police began assaulting seated protesters. Often, defenders of Antifa militancy call the resort to violent tactics a form of self-defense—a preemptive act to protect the community from the violence inherent to fascist organizing. When Antifa protesters aggressively shut down Milo Yiannopoulos's talk at Berkeley, numerous participants cited the bigot's tendency to use his platform to name and out transgender students on campus. After Charlottesville, Dr. Cornel West, who marched that day with local clergy, said of Antifa: "They saved our lives, actually. We would have been completely crushed." Of the white supremacists, on the other hand, he remarked, "I've never seen that kind of hatred in my life."

We must delineate what we are, and are not, willing to name "violence." I don't believe a smashed bank window or a burning trash can on the Berkeley campus outside a Milo speech to be victims of violence or to produce victims. But that is not an absolute distinction related to animate versus inanimate objects—for a smashed mosque window or a swastika on a Jewish grave would, by my lights, produce legitimate victims of violence. The latter, but not the former, are in service of an ideology—white supremacy—in which violence inheres. There is a crucial distinction between destruction as collateral damage of a political end (say, in the goal of disrupting a neo-Nazi gathering), versus as its central tenet (genocide).

Anti-fascist violence is thus a counterviolence, not an instigation of violence onto a terrain of preexisting peace. A situation in which fascists can gather to preach hate and chant "blood and soil"—this is a background state of violence. The problem we face, then, is not so much that of *necessary violence* as it is one of *impossible nonviolence*.

The next obvious question pertains to targets: Where does one draw the line concerning which groups or speakers deserve anti-fascist exposure and confrontation? We might agree when it comes to openly white nationalist activists—the Richard Spencers or Nathan Damigos of the world—but what of someone like racist pseudoscientist Charles Murray, or members of the so-called "alt-lite" who purport to not be racist, but who run in the same circles? There's no Antifa committee or council that draws rules to serve as rails about who counts as fascist enough to fight; each community that takes anti-fascist action must decide for itself on appropriate targets and tactics. This constitutes an ethical practice, not a moral code. And it's worth noting that this is largely a hypothetical concern: it has not posed a problem that Antifa activists have gone after "regular" Trump supporters. Perhaps some college Republicans had their "Make America Great Again" hats unceremoniously knocked off at Berkeley, but they were organizing and supporting a Milo talk. And this is the Antifa point: to make consequences felt for organizing with or alongside white supremacists and hatemongers.

Slippery slope arguments are distractions at a time when there are so many outright-fascist organizations at which to aim our anti-fascism.

Fascism is not just a type of regime, nor is it an ideology for a would-be regime. As noted above, micro-fascisms permeate quotidian life, as does the perverted desire for fascism. But the practical question of where to draw the line when it comes to deploying violent counterprotest has not been answered. (We do not, for example, do the work of anti-fascisting ourselves by punching ourselves in the face daily—or at least I don't —but then again, we are not seeking to organize with proactively fascist racists as a form of life). Borrowing from Italian novelist and critic Umberto Eco, we might want to use the term "ur-fascist" for those for whom violent intervention could be an ethical possibility.

I can't give you a definition of ur-fascism that accounts for every instance of something we might want to call ur-fascism in the world, any more than I can give you a definition of the term "game" that covers every instance of something we correctly call a game. This was what philosopher Ludwig Wittgenstein meant by a "family resemblance concept"—there is no one essential common feature shared by all things we call "game"; rather we see "a complicated network of similarities overlapping and crisscrossing." I'm not the first to apply the idea to fascism. Eco wrote in the *New York Review of Books* that "fascism is not unlike Wittgenstein's notion of a game," noting, "Fascism became an all-purpose term because one can eliminate from a fascist regime one or more features, and it will still be recognizable as fascist." So we might name an overlapping network of similarities like populism, nationalism, racism, traditionalism and disregard for reasoned debate— any one (or more) of these could be absent, and the term "ur-fascism" would still apply.

But I'd suggest that we can further use Wittgenstein's family resemblance idea to talk about whether we draw the boundary on what counts as an ur-fascist. Wittgenstein talks about the problem of delineating the boundaries of a term or concept thus:

> I can give the concept "number" rigid limits … that is, use the word "number" for a rigidly limited concept, but I can also use it so that the extension of the concept is not closed by a frontier. And this is how we do use the word "game". For how is the concept of a game bounded? What still counts as a game and what no longer does? Can you give the boundary? No. You can draw one; for none has so far been drawn. (But that never troubled you before when you used the word "game".)

So I cannot give you the boundary of ur-fascism, or the clear path away from fascism; we, in practice, have to draw it as we go. Understandably, that is a more troubling conclusion than when this logic is applied to the use of the word "game." But this is where ethics comes in: collective decision making, community inclusion, and careful but forceful deliberation about what (or who) counts as a threat when they attempt to take platforms or to organize in our midst.

Toward anti-fascisting, even while we cannot anti-fascist be!

2

Ghost Stories

If you have ghosts, you have everything
—Roky Erickson

C: *Someone has died who is not dead*
M: *And now we are friends*
—Sarah Kane, *Crave* (1998)

I don't see dead people. But a ghost has haunted the bathroom adjoined to my childhood bedroom for as long as I can
remember, and it terrifies me. I don't believe in ghosts.

I was around seven years old when my family moved to
the leafy 1930s-style detached home in London in which my
parents still live. My bedroom was on the back corner of the
second floor, with an en suite bathroom. It boasted a dusty
pink tub and toilet, installed when avocado green was an
acceptable bathroom color scheme. I don't trace the ghost
back to that era, or to any specific time. All I know is that he
was there when, or as, I arrived. I have never been haunted—
except metaphorically—anywhere else.

This ghost is formless—a shadow that seems to peer back,
an aspect that shifts when you look back twice, a displacer
of air in the room. I've feared him for as long as I've disbe-
lieved in his broader kind. A few months ago, I was back to
London to stay in that house with my boyfriend, to whom
I clung throughout the night in fear. I wasn't afraid that the
ghost might come; the ghost was already there. It's not a heavy
presence all night, but he stirs at some point or points most

nights. The bathroom shifts from small and quaint to a cave of darkness visible. Closing the bathroom door doesn't help; the concealment can evoke more dread.

There is no prima facie contradiction in fearing something that one does not believe to exist. This experience is not even an unusual one—a fact attested to by the success of horror movies. My fear doesn't point to a de facto belief, and the ghost who haunts my childhood bathroom does not present grounds for shifting my web of ontological commitments to include a realm of formerly embodied souls wandering among us. I'm not simply waiting for the right empirical experience to substantiate a coherent and comprehensible ghost world for me. But the least interesting thing to do with my ghost is to explain him away.

Instead, I want to account for my ghost without reducing him to nonexistence or empirical fact. Rather than as a mere metaphor, I want to insist upon the ghost's presence as a substantive reminder to believe and disbelieve differently—to believe and disbelieve simultaneously, with a commitment that goes beyond a jump in the night. The *hows*, not the *whats*, by which he is. I aim to explain why I can allow a certain reality of the ghost—and why I should, and you should too.

I was petrified as a child, but only in private. Neither withdrawn nor fanciful, I was not imaginative enough to see ghosts everywhere, nor fairies anywhere. And if I was precocious enough to reject magic, I was not philosophical enough, until much later, to let it back in. But my bathroom was haunted.

The haunting was pretty standard: I would lie like stone under my covers, hiding my feet. Trips to pee at night were mad dashes to the toilet and back, under the watch of a dark presence, with a felt immateriality no less robust than a human gaze. Yes, yes, the male gaze in my bathroom mirror. The fact that the ghost has always seemed male to me is probably not an accident, but this essay isn't a therapy session. The ghost will never show or prove itself male or not, or gendered in any direction, because the ghost won't prove itself at all. And the ghost hardly stands alone in the set of beings interpellated through gender. But, again, the ghost is not a metaphor.

As children often are, I was better back then at maintaining contradictions—the reality and unreality of the ghost was no mental strain. But I contracted positivism while growing up, and I tried to explain my ghost away. When I was around eleven, a physics teacher accidentally offered some bright relief by describing the phenomenon of sleep paralysis, when a person experiences a total inability to move or speak while on the edge of waking, a state often accompanied by visual and auditory hallucinations, and the sense that a presence is physically weighing on them or the edge of the bed. Centuries of succubus and incubus demons sitting on chests, all explained as a glitch on the journey to or from REM sleep.

A bad drug trip can be mitigated by the reminder that it's drug-induced. Hallucinations, deciphered as mental illness, can be mitigated by the use of drugs. In both cases, what matters is an intervention that asserts that the hallucination is not real. Such reality-affirming (or -inscribing) interventions can be lifesaving. The same considerations need not apply to my ghost. While he could be explained merely as the product of sleep paralysis, the simplest explanation is not always the best. The explanation you choose for a phenomenon partly depends on your aims. Knowing about sleep paralysis didn't stop it occurring, nor did it vanquish the ghost as an ongoing presence to this day.

When my mother told me that she uses my bathroom and bedroom for my baby nephew when he stays over, I shuddered. My nephew's little body, bubble bath, baby toys, and the ghost. I leave psychic room for the possibility that they might notice each other.

Although I'm the only one who has experienced my bathroom ghost, he is not a private mental object. (I don't believe in private mental objects.) I talk about the ghost now, joke about him. I'm telling you about my ghost because I don't really know how to tell about him. I point to him here, because I can't but I do. If he (or anything) were just a subjective phenomenological experience, we wouldn't be able to discuss it. Sure, you can't feel what it feels like to be haunted by my ghost, but you also can't feel what it is like to be me in general. That's not unique to haunting, and it is not a good enough reason to dismiss the ghost as just an invention of my imagination. Equally, if the ghost were simply *there*—like standard-issue worldly stuff—there'd be no grounds for comment, no reason to reach out and share him with you. It's his ambiguity that makes him worth mention.

Intimacy lives in those places we don't reduce to the wholly explicable, even though we could.

Contemporary science allows for the reality of my ghost only insofar as he is the content of a real hallucination or psychological process, steeped in my projections. And I can't disagree with that conclusion, aside from the fact that it's not much fun. My disagreement begins with the assertion that hallucination or imagination are the *only* possible terrains of reality for my ghost.

The new atheists, such as evolutionary biologist Richard Dawkins, or social critics Christopher Hitchens and Sam Harris—the worst of all ghostbusters—demand the universe, however physically massive, be as small and legible as possible. They would do well to consult some better empiricists. Willard Van Orman Quine, a twentieth-century American logician and philosopher, had little time for ghosts, but even less time for the sort of bad thinking that organizes the world into stable, immovable categories that could never allow for ghosts. Quine thought our theories of the world should be considered webs of belief, with centers and peripheries. At the center of the web are propositions we might call analytically true, or a priori—for instance, 2 + 2 = 4; or *all bachelors are unmarried*. On the periphery are beliefs that can be changed based on some recalcitrant experiences; for example, if one believes there are no red-haired French people, but then meets a few red-haired French people, the original belief is easily revised. Quine rejected that these are actually two different types of truth, epistemologically (i.e., really). Given the right, albeit dramatic, alterations to a belief web, 2 + 2 = 4 could be false, and not just by swapping around the meaning of words.

Right now, as I sit here soberly typing, if I see a pink elephant dance into the room, my web of belief is such that I assume I am hallucinating, not that pink elephants dance into rooms. It would take a decent dose of recalcitrant evidence for me to choose the latter explanation. Given that we develop these holistic systems in societal, not isolated, contexts, it would likely take a critical mass of people experiencing the pink elephant to conclude that the pink-elephant hypothesis is a better story of reality than the hallucination hypothesis. But Quine's point is that this is possible.

Webs of belief are holistic systems, and they can shift to include new, even radical propositions, so long as the entire web shifts accordingly. The webs of belief aren't intersubjective attempts to map out a real world—that is, a map that gets closer and closer to truth with better and better science. Rather, they delineate reality at a given time, and every proposition contained in such a web is (in theory) revisable. They could shift to include the existence of ghosts, or just one bathroom ghost. We can imagine a world in which we had enough shared experiences to include bathroom ghosts as verifiable objects in our web of belief. More crucially, Quine's approach entails not only that we could "add" ghosts to the set of existing things, but also that we can maintain webs of belief in which things do and don't exist at the same time.

A given web of belief is better, by Quine's empiricist lights, if it better predicts future phenomena based on experience.

But, using the example of Homer's gods, he noted that the affective reality of something doesn't depend on its materiality: "In point of epistemological footing," Quine wrote, "the physical objects and the gods differ only in degree and not in kind. Both sorts of entities enter our conceptions only as cultural posits."

This points to the larger stakes of Quinean holism, which relate to my ghost's mode of existence. When Quine talked about conceptual schemes for future prediction, he failed to talk about desire, about ethics. In affirming my ghost, I'm asking that we not be boring assholes about what gets to exist, and how. The ghost invites an ethical consideration, not just an ontological one: he is indicative of inexplicable possibilities, which get ruled out as empirically impossible. We act better, I believe, when we don't work to fold every unusual phenomenon into a preexisting dogma. It's a political imperative to believe (impossibly) that another world is possible, while necessarily being unable to explain that world from the confines of this one. The "inexpressible contained—inexpressibly! —in the expressed," as literary scholar and author Maggie Nelson summed up Wittgenstein's central concern in her 2015 book *The Argonauts*.

The Babadook (2014), for example, is such a good movie because it refuses to reduce its monster to a psychological posit. We realize we are watching the story of a mother and a son haunted by grief, but the film insists, too, that the monster, qua monster, is real. The Babadook isn't banished to the psyche, but to the basement—and all the better for the universe of the film.

In my web of belief, my bathroom ghost sits somewhere liminal; he's not part of how I typically navigate the world, which requires constant banal prediction. That it remains there, however, is ethically important. Your ghosts, too, your demons, your holy visions, don't need to exist; you could no doubt account for them scientifically. The bombastic tendency of Western science is to pathologize, and thus to dismiss such things. But the question of what realities are possible should not just be answered by the measurable components of what already has been. Does maintaining the reality of your ghost hurt you or help you? Does a collective commitment to something mystical, outside "reason," cause more harm than good? My bathroom ghost is a heuristic (again, not a metaphor) for considering what is desirable to allow in our worlds as opposed to that which we should explain away. Because even though I *could* explain him away, he will still come and scare me. So I might as well make epistemic room for him; it's more interesting to do so.

Ontologies are open ethical questions we have to ask again and again. This is no more true of, say, religious ontological commitments than it is of the sciences that foolishly believe themselves to have escaped ideology.

A few decades ago, there was a critical theory trend for making use of ghosts. Deconstructionist philosopher Jacques Derrida introduced the idea of "hauntology" (which, by no accident, sounds exactly like "ontology" in his native French pronunciation) as a radical critique in order to use temporality to challenge the limits of totalities and ideological dichotomies. Insofar as we always live with presence and nonpresence, he suggests, there are spirits. We see this clearly in fiction: all stories are ghost stories, in which reading invokes a return to the present of specters—say, a dead writer, or an idea from the past. Derrida, for his part, focused on the examples of Marx's "specter of communism" and Shakespeare's principal tragedy. Tenses are muddled; "The time is out of joint," says Hamlet. These hauntings occupy an ambiguous ontology between life and death, presence and absence. "They are always there, specters, even if they do not exist, even if they are no longer, even if they are not yet," Derrida wrote. "Haunting is the state of proper being as such."

Though "to be or not to be" remains *Hamlet*'s most quoted phrase, in the play's broader context, life or death is not the question at all. The dichotomy is undone from the beginning. For the play begins with a ghost, the king who is and is not —both gone and present, both rightful king and no-longer king. Hamlet fails to understand the hauntological universe in which he lives, where "to be or not to be" fails to exhaust the logical space.

I like the thought, but Derrida's intervention in ideological totality seems to posit an ossified world of haunting itself. It reminds me of Henrik Ibsen's play *Ghosts*, and his tormented Mrs. Alving, who says,

> I am half inclined to think we are all ghosts ... It is not only what we have inherited from our fathers and mothers that exists again in us, but all sorts of old dead ideas and all kinds of old dead beliefs and things of that kind. They are not actually alive in us; but there they are dormant all the same, and we can never be rid of them.

For Derrida, the possibility of something dead-and-alive, so neither dead nor alive, ruptures notions of a world ordered into presence and absence. We would do well, unlike Hamlet, to notice it.

Derrida's ghosts that put time out of joint shouldn't be so strange to us digital denizens. We live with and through digital selves, and we are beyond the era in which online experiences and relations were deemed and experienced as "unreal." We have normalized the fact of our enmeshed digital existences and expanded what we allow to be "real" selves, real experiences. How the internet functions is wholly explicable— there's no spectral mystery as to how we integrate into networks—but just how our phenomenology has accommodated them is a magic of sorts. It evidences our ability to relate in ways once deemed unreal. It took collective leaps of faith to see online avatars as aspects of people rather than simply pictures of them, to feel an iPhone as a bodily extension. "There you are!" I say as a friend goes green on Google Hangouts. We've shifted the possibilities of "there" and "where" a whole lot in recent decades. We don't call digitally integrated life "mystical" or "paranormal"; tech companies would rather we simply call it "progress" and reap the profits for themselves.

Still, it took choice and a certain consensus (albeit hierarchically organized by Silicon Valley technocapital) to permit digital reality to become real. That choice was simultaneously one to introduce ambiguity into the real; otherwise, "IRL" would make no sense as a phrase. My ghost is possible by the same logic, although, to his credit, he will not find articulation through capitalist enterprise.

Remember the dress? The optical illusion, which seemed to split the internet into two camps in early 2015—those who saw one color scheme on a photographed cocktail dress and those who saw another. Gold and white, or blue and black—and maddening either way. Like Wittgenstein's duck/rabbit perception puzzle in which both a duck and a rabbit can be seen, depending on how you look at it (and which, by the by, I have tattooed on my arm), the dress was an aspect perception game: one reading of the image makes the other (equally valid) reading impossible to see. Unlike the duck/rabbit, where most people manage to see both duck and rabbit, the dress was less available for aspect shifting. Most people could only ever see either the gold and white, or the blue and black. We couldn't force ourselves to alternate between them, even as we begged each other to try to see it our way. Scientific explanations of the phenomena were given, but it didn't matter, I was a gold-and-white; it didn't open to me the blue-black aspect. Fuck what the dress looked like in the store—in the viral image we shared, a blue and black dress and a gold and white dress both simultaneously existed, while neither existed at once. And what fun with that we had!

For Wittgenstein, the point about aspect perception is that it is neither through "the language game of reporting" nor "the language game of information" that such phenomena are best read. The least interesting thing about the dress was that it was actually blue and black, while the explanation of why different aspects can be seen is perhaps equally impertinent. To talk of an aspect's truth or falsity misses the point, and that is precisely what's important about these figures. Perception is not just the expression of a subjective experience, but goes beyond the personal: we ask each other, compel each other, to perceive an aspect of an object or an experience that has struck us. There's an intimacy in inviting each other to perceive anew, to accept the invitation, and to be taken by surprise. We wish to be struck together with, in Wittgenstein's phrase, an "inarticulate reverberate of a thought." This closeness is about sharing realities beyond the reach of plain or obvious empirical experience. For if reality is *just there*, then we all exist together in its sameness, separately and alone, with ghosts no more than metaphors.

Riots for Black Life

For less than one week in the summer of 2011, London blazed with riots, which sprawled throughout the capital and the nation. Police had shot dead Mark Duggan, an unarmed twenty-nine-year-old, prompting an eruption of property damage (an estimated $3.5 million worth), arson, and looting. Tabloid ink ran sticky with panic and racist, classist allusions to roaming packs of hooligans. The police cracked down hard: five days of chaos produced 3,100 arrests. The courts followed suit, jailing one student for six months simply for looting bottles of water, worth around five dollars, from a grocery chain.

And then there were the brooms. In the wake of the unrest, hundreds of well-meaning British civilians took to the streets, armed with brooms, to voluntarily sweep away the debris of the preceding rage-filled days. Keep calm and carry on. The organizers dubbed it "the great clean up"—a blunt puritanical assertion that goodness, nay greatness, fell on the side of the largely white, middle-class citizens who would wipe clean the charred evidence of social strife left by the underclasses.

Subsequent in-depth studies by the London School of Economics and the *Guardian* found structural racism, classism, and habitual police brutality to be among driving forces of the riotous rupture. But at the time, a pernicious narrative emerged that pitted "criminal," "violent" rioters against the upstanding broom brigade who swept away the mess. While then–prime minister David Cameron called the riots "criminality, pure and simple," there was nothing pure nor simple about the events of that August week. And wrongheaded politicians are not alone in seeking to reduce messy and complex events like mass riots into the "pure and simple" categories of "criminality" and order, violence and peace, goodies and baddies.

We saw a similar line play out during the August 2014 events in Ferguson, Missouri, after police officer Darren Wilson shot dead unarmed, Black eighteen-year-old Michael Brown. Wilson claimed the teen tried to attack him in his car and grab his gun, but eyewitnesses countered this narrative, reporting that Brown was in fact surrendering, hands in the air, when he was shot. Brown's body lay in the street for four hours before being removed. The protest cries went up: *Hands up; don't shoot*; *Black lives matter*.

The St. Louis suburb was hit by rioting, looting, and confrontations with militarized cops. Clashes with police and property destruction continued for over a week, erupting anew when a grand jury failed to indict Officer Wilson. The official and media narratives around Brown's execution, his killer's impunity, and the furious protests that followed epitomized the (im)moral undergirding of American necropolitics—specifically, the demonization and decimation of Black life.

Later that month, the *New York Times* published an outrage-provoking obituary describing Brown as "no angel." The author felt the need to note that the teen—as teens do—would sometimes drink alcohol and smoke weed, and that Brown once got into a fight. "He did not have a criminal record as an adult, and his family said he never got in trouble with the law as a juvenile, either," the article noted. With just over a thousand words to reflect on Brown's whole life, an entire sentence was dedicated to the absence of a rap sheet. It would seem bizarre, except within a context that presumed the a priori guilt of Black boys as a baseline—which was, of course, the very context of Brown's death.

The paper's public editor criticized the "no angel" designation, but it wouldn't be the last instance in which Brown's assigned place in the divine order would play a role in the narrative surrounding his death. Following the announcement that Wilson would not go to trial, the St. Louis county prosecutor made the unorthodox decision to release the grand jury testimony records to the public. The alleged gesture toward transparency only served to reveal a mistake-riddled process, in which judgment was passed not so much over Wilson's culpability, but over his victim's very soul. The grand jury heard from the officer that when he shot the teen, Brown's face (which the cop described as an "it") looked like a "demon."

The literal demonization of Brown as a justification for his killing echoed the white supremacist tradition of reliance on the constructed figure of the Black devil—a character accorded not only circumstantial, but also divine and existential guilt. Thus, it must not be taken lightly that a white man, endowed by the state with firepower and authority, used the term "demon" to defend ending the life of an unarmed Black teenager. In a sixteenth-century English myth, the devil would take the shape of the Black Moor; and in 1584, Reginald Scot's famous skeptical text, *The Discoverie of Witchcraft*, noted the contemporary belief that "a damned soule may and dooth take the shape of a black moore."

In *Othello*, written circa 1604, Shakespeare's most villainous creation, Iago, warns the white Venetian senator Brabantio that the "devil will make a grandsire" of him if Othello, the Moor, is permitted to marry and procreate with his white daughter. It was the same racist allusions of Jacobean religious paranoia that found purchase in that Ferguson grand jury meeting room. And the paper of record joined the demonizing chorus, upholding a narrative that stood on the shoulders of centuries of wretched racism.

~

37

A related moralization concerned the riots that followed, with angels and demons projected onto well-worn good-protester/bad-protester dichotomies. This played out, too, in Baltimore in 2015, when Black twenty-five-year-old Freddie Gray died in custody. His spinal cord had been snapped during a "rough ride" in a police van. After countless police killings of young Black people, even the response to furious, righteous protest has become predictable. The protests, we are told, "turn violent." Racists and reactionaries call it thuggery (pure and simple). Liberals, believing themselves on the right side of the anti-racist struggle, condemn the "violent" protesters, and stress the presence of good, nonviolent demonstrators, who marched and mourned but didn't riot or loot.

With their desire to rescue uprisings from a demonizing narrative of violence and criminality, liberal voices (albeit unwittingly) performed their own violent categorization. Vicky Osterweil put it best in an essay for the *New Inquiry* after the Ferguson revolt in 2014:

> When protesters proclaim that "not all protesters were looters, in fact, most of the looters weren't part of the protest!" or words to that effect, they are trying to fight a horrifically racist history of Black people depicted in American culture as robbers and thieves: Precisely the image that the Ferguson police tried to evoke to assassinate Michael Brown's character and justify his killing post facto. It is a completely righteous and understandable position.
>
> However, in trying to correct this media image—in making a strong division between Good Protesters and Bad Rioters, or between ethical non-violence practitioners and supposedly violent looters—the narrative of the criminalization of Black youth is reproduced. This time it delineates certain kinds of Black youth—those who loot versus those who protest. The effect of this discourse is hardening a permanent category of criminality on Black subjects who produce a supposed crime within the context of a protest.

38

Osterweil's crucial defense of rioting was not a condemnation of the historic contributions of activists engaging in disciplined nonviolence in the tradition of MLK. Rather, she stresses the central role of nonviolent civil disobedience in civil rights struggle, while still rejecting a view that counterposes those who riot and loot as the "bad protesters" failing an otherwise-righteous movement. Rioting is not senseless destruction; on the contrary, it is often (even without explicit intention) a deeply political challenge to property and white supremacy —two concepts intractably entwined in this former slave-holder republic. Only when rendered in the language of capital are the acts of smashing chain store and cop car windows sufficient to see a protest deemed "violent"; but this is the media lingua franca.

Liberal commentary on riots, especially on those carried out by young, Black and poor people, often becomes hypercritical of the choice of targets of damage. There is marginally more sympathy for the act of smashing a Walmart window than a local mom-and-pop setup. Certainly, I'd rather see a retail giant, famed for worker abuses, smashed and burned than I would a small, local business. But above that, I also privilege the political force of a riot over the preservation of shop windows. Collective fury, inscribed onto urban terrain in the form of property damage, can be an assertion of presence and power in the face of authorities who would rather these young people remain invisible, silenced, imprisoned or dead. The disruption and destruction says it all, and it needs little accounting for in this instance. Revolutionary theorist Frantz Fanon put it well in his 1961 *Wretched of the Earth*: "When we revolt it's not for a particular culture. We revolt simply because we can no longer breathe."

Looting was an obsessive focus of coverage during the 1992 Los Angeles riots following the brutal police beating of Rodney King, as well as during the 2011 London riots and amid the brief but intense unrest in Brooklyn's East Flatbush in 2013, after cops shot dead sixteen-year-old Kimani Gray. And while it would be easy to demonize looters here, in order to preserve some sort of ideological purity for those vandals who destroy in righteous anger alone, I'll leave it to David Cameron to deem things "pure and simple." For the reality is that looting adds a complicated layer to questions about the ethics of rioting.

Arguments that looters distract focus from rage at killer cops may be valid. But I submit, along with Osterweil, that the very media venues that are so keen to condemn rioting and looting would have paid little attention to a St. Louis suburb's polite protest of the latest racist police killing. If the public has more concern for the well-being of people than of property, as I hope they do, consternation about looting should pale in comparison to anger at police violence. Both liberals and conservatives decry looting as opportunistic, but I'm not sure opportunism is always such a bad thing, especially for individuals and communities for whom opportunity rarely comes knocking.

On the night that the Ferguson QuikTrip convenience store was gutted by fire after being looted, DeAndre Smith, a thirty-year-old local resident, told the *St. Louis Post-Dispatch* what the destruction meant to him: "This is exactly what's supposed to happen when an injustice is happening in your community. When you have kids getting killed for nothing … I don't think it's over. I think they just got a taste of what fighting back means."

To tell a furious community that their riotous actions are counterproductive patronizes the very groups who know too well that "acceptable channels" of political engagement have failed, again and again, to deliver dignity and justice to Black life. Further, it ignores, as Osterweil notes, that major riots (and the threat of more) during the civil rights era helped force JFK's hand in calling for historic legislation: "To argue that the movement achieved what it did in spite of rather than as a result of the mixture of not-nonviolent and nonviolent action is spurious at best."

The wave of Black Lives Matter protests—catalyzed by events in Ferguson but fueled by years of police killing Black youth with impunity—was remarkable in size, scope, and resilience. Without central planning, and eschewing the defanged respectability politics of elder statesmen and politicians calling for calm, these protests consistently shared the aim crystallized in the hashtag #ShutItDown. As movement journalist L. A. Kauffman pointed out in a December 2014 article in the *Baffler*, although protesters have in the past "used their bodies to block bridges, tunnels, intersections, and roadways," the amount of "spontaneous and simultaneous disruptive action" we saw during these mobilizations was unprecedented.

When more than 700 Occupy Wall Street participants blocked the Brooklyn Bridge in late 2011, it made headlines around the country. I was there and felt that weighted rush of something significant happening as, for just a few hours, bodies disrupted the ordinary flows on that great stone artery above the East River.

That was a few hours on one drizzling October afternoon. During the most visible days of protests for Black lives, major infrastructure was blocked nightly, and often in more than one place at the same time. On one December night in 2014, following the failure of a New York grand jury to indict the cop who choked Eric Garner to death, demonstrations blocked the I-93 entrance in Boston, the 110 Freeway in Los Angeles, I-80 in Berkeley, and every major highway, bridge and tunnel in and out of Lower Manhattan. A traffic map of New York City, highlighting jams in red, looked like a heart pumping blood.

Blocking infrastructure turns a demonstration of collective anger into a manifestation. Planned and permitted protest parades, however large, are folded into the ordinary metab-olism of city business. March routes are delineated; traffic, while slowed, is smoothly redirected and at the end of the day, traffic and commerce buzzes along as if nothing ever happened. The largest climate march in history was held in Manhattan in September 2014 and amounted to little more than a grand parade. Parades are scheduled in the city every year. Disruptions, by definition, are not. Not every disruption is a riot, but most every riot is a disruption.

Beyond questions of justifying riots, a categorical error is made in any narrative resting on the idea of a violent "turn" in such protests. The very idea of a demonstration like those in Ferguson "turning violent"—as it was described in standard media parlance—mislocated and thus misframed violence in this context.

The error exists in the tacit suggestion that there was a sit-uation of nonviolence, or peace, from which to turn. To be clear: any circumstance in which cops take Black life with impunity, any context in which it is still necessary to state that Black Lives Matter, is a background state of constant violence.

Riotous protesters do not bring violence; the violence was there in the DNA of white supremacy and our world through which it permeates. Protester violence here is counterviolence in history's unbroken dialectic of violence and countervio-lence. Even a rhetoric of police turning violent during a specific protest ignores that policing, as an institution in this country, functions as a force of consistent violence against Black life. And more often than not, cops' roles as violent instigators are erased from media narratives. The malignant euphemism "officer involved shooting" says it all.

But even in the rare moments, as during the beginning days of the Ferguson uprising, when a show of militarized policing draws public outrage, it tends to be the bellicose spec-tacle of tanks and smoke that draws ire. Quotidian policing is not marked as a violence, and law enforcement is praised when protests are contained and calm. When effective police crowd control—the avoidance of major property damage, the minimal disruption of business and traffic, de-escalation of intensity—gets celebrated as the maintenance of peace, the myth perpetuates that we have a baseline state of peace, peppered with violent turns. Which may ring true for America's white and privileged. But the lie is exposed, overexposed, glaring: people who have to assert that their lives matter exist in a state of constant violence. As political activist and scholar Angela Davis said in a 1972 interview, "If you are a Black person and live in the Black community all your life and walk out on the street every day seeing white policemen surrounding you … And when you live under a situation like that constantly, and then you ask me, you know, whether I approve of violence. I mean, that just doesn't make any sense at all."

The institutions and vectors of white supremacy have never turned from structural violence. Yet the media consistently attributes the act of turning to violence to people who literally cannot turn from it; whose lives and deaths are organized by it. Why not end the cycle? A better question: is it not cruel to demand peace from those who are not permitted to live in it? I repeat here the words of late philosopher Bernard Williams, who noted that "to say peace when there is no peace is to say nothing." In Ferguson and Baltimore, with smashed glass and fire, something was said.

4

Homegrown

In late May of 2020, Minneapolis police officer Derek Chauvin, surrounded by three supportive colleagues, knelt on the neck of George Floyd for nearly nine minutes. Pinned facedown on the street, the 46-year-old Black father of five begged, "Please, man!" Bystanders implored the officers to "let him breathe." One shouted, "He is a human being!" With his last breath, Floyd cried out, "Momma!" and then, "Momma, I'm through." He lay motionless, dying, for two minutes before Chauvin lifted his knee.

Floyd had been detained for allegedly trying to use a counterfeit twenty-dollar bill at a grocery store; like millions of others during the coronavirus pandemic, he'd lost his job earlier in the year. He had himself contracted and recovered from Covid-19 the month before his execution.

One day after Floyd's death, footage of which garnered swift viral attention, crowds flooded the streets of Minneapolis and Saint Paul. On the third day of raging protests, a contingent of rebels besieged the Minneapolis Police Department's Third Precinct. In retreat, the cops abandoned the building, and by the next morning, it was a gutted, charred shell.

What an act: to burn down the edifice of a seemingly impenetrable force—the same force that had days before, without compunction, turned a Black man into a corpse. I watched the precinct burn via livestream video on Twitter. In the foreground, silhouetted by the flames, hundreds celebrated.

Protests spread quickly across the country, with undulating levels of ferocity. The next night in Brooklyn, I joined thousands in the streets. The days and nights that followed were filled with furious marches led by young Black New Yorkers in every borough. Even in this city, under the gaze of the largest police force in the world, NYPD vehicles were burned and luxury stores were looted.

The riots not only represented the boldest popular abolitionist expression in at least a generation; they also marked a jolting rupture in pandemic-era isolation. "All riots emit a world-historical shine, but the George Floyd uprisings were extra radiant because they opened the doors of the world," artist and writer Hannah Black reflected. "The riots saved social life by proving that it was possible, with masks and moving air, to spend time together outdoors without getting sick." This context must not be overlooked: Black people and other people of color have been contracting and dying from the coronavirus at rates far higher than white people. The vast revolt came in the midst of this pandemic, which has only further revealed and exacerbated the deadly hierarchies of our white supremacist order.

At the time, we did not fully know the relatively low risk of contagion while moving outdoors, especially in masks; what we did know was the extreme threat posed to Black life by the plague of policing. As ever, but for new reasons, masks and mutual aid helped keep rebels safe. Life spread through the furious crowds; the virus did not.

Extreme state repression reliably followed, with brutal policing of protests leading to thousands of arrests. Defanging liberal calls for "peaceful protest" rang out, as did condemnations of property destruction as violence. The militancy of the first weeks of uprising gave way to long and predictable mass marches. But those eruptive nights in early June were the most powerful challenges to the city's racist bastions—policing and the property it protects—that I have ever witnessed.

Within two days of Floyd's murder, as the protests spread nationwide, Trump signaled his strategy to invoke "Antifa" to undermine the uprisings as the work of "outside agitators," while further encouraging and legitimizing law enforcement crackdowns and white supremacist vigilantism. As is typical, he did so with a most Trumpian tweet: "The United States of America will be designating ANTIFA as a Terrorist Organization." The statement combined a profound ignorance of—or disregard for—the official mechanisms of US governance, a deep connection to the mentality of his white supremacist base, a desire to distract and distort, and an authoritarian confidence (grimly justified) in the political consequences of his raging online proclamations.

Of course, the president could not, in one fell tweet, shift the legal status of anti-fascist activity or Antifa affiliations. Needless to repeat that no centralized Antifa "organization" exists. Nor is there any US statute under which groups are designated domestic terror organizations. Nonetheless, federal law enforcement uses domestic terrorism categories to organize and describe cases, and a host of anti-terrorism laws are available for use against "domestic extremists." Trump's tweet was by no means meaningless. Dozens of protest arrestees around the country reported being questioned during their detention about Antifa connections, often by clueless federal agents tasked with producing a reality to match the Trumpian mythology of Antifa "terror."

With the cynical invocation of "Antifa," politicians from the far right to the centrist liberal sought to discredit Black rebellion, while laying the ground for ever more brutal anti-Black repression. Since no formal Antifa organization exists, the label provided an expansive-enough cover for a wide range of crackdowns and retaliations against any number of protesters. Trump blamed "ANTIFA," and Attorney General Bill Barr followed up by stating that the Justice Department planned to use its network of fifty-six regional FBI Joint Terrorism Task Forces to identify the "criminal organizers and instigators," while specifically naming "antifa and other similar groups."

Even though the term was largely an empty signifier in the scope of the Black-led uprisings, such finger-pointing served as a tool to unleash the weight of federal law enforcement against Black protest, while rhetorically denying Black agency.

It is a historical racist trope to suggest that Black communities could not rise up and self-organize huge revolutionary action. In every major city, it was abundantly clear that the uprisings were being led by young Black people. The promulgation of outside-agitator myths erased the agency of those communities organizing on the front lines. This divide-and-conquer strategy is as old and tired as any "bad protester versus good protester" dyad, which time and again has distracted from the glut of police violence attending every moment of anti-racist protest.

It just so happens that this strategy was also favored by the Ku Klux Klan. In the 1930s, the Klan issued flyers in Alabama stating that "paid organizers for the communists are only trying" to get Black people "in trouble." As James Baldwin wrote in 1961, "It is a notion which contains a gratuitous insult implying, as it does," that Black people "can make no move unless they are manipulated."

When Trump railed against Antifa and "radical-left anarchists," the assumption was clearly that these so-called infiltrators were to be imagined as white. There is little doubt that white anarchists and self-identifying Antifa activists took part in the 2020 protests and, at times, took militant action. But having been involved in anarchist organizing in the United States for a decade, I can assure you that there are simply far too few explicitly anarchist or Antifa activists (white or non-white) to account for the vast scope of insurrectionary activity that took place over those weeks. And, more to the point, the Black people taking radical action have no need for white leftist instigation.

Politicians like New York mayor Bill de Blasio also blamed "anarchists" and "Antifa" for the riotous protests in their cities, tacitly suggesting that a furious eruption against the constant violence exerted against Black life would be somehow illegitimate or inexplicable—that it must have come from outside. Not to mention that most of the "outside agitator" claims were provably false. Minnesota governor Tim Walz said that 81 percent of protest arrestees in the first days of the uprisings were not locals; however, numerous press reports found that over 80 percent of arrestees had local addresses. As Austin-based anarchist scott crow wrote in early June, "Blaming anarchists and antifa, with absolutely no evidence, is a way to make what's happening seem fringe and marginal when these are popular uprisings ... This is a time of mass outrage at an unjust system."

The uprisings were not ignited through infiltration by Antifa cells, but they are accurately described as anti-fascist. "Antifa," after all, is not *only* a shortening of "anti-fascist," but speaks to a set of radical practices inherited through a particular historical trajectory and tradition—one with European origins. The driving anti-fascist force behind the 2020 uprisings was born of a different legacy, that of militant Black resistance in this country. So when Trump, his servile Justice Department, and numerous Republicans and Democrats were swift to blame Antifa and "outside agitators" for inciting unrest, it was an erasure of the anti-fascism endogenous to Black liberation struggle.

Trump-led efforts to discredit the uprisings as the work of Antifa unwittingly highlighted the importance of reorienting our frameworks of anti-fascism in the United States to center its legacy in the Black radical tradition. In doing so, we can better appreciate the sui generis nature of American fascism in a way that makes clear, in no uncertain terms, that fascism in this country was not undone with the unseating of Trump, nor is it simply a question of battling far-right organizations and individuals. Its shock troops and structures, to say nothing of its core constituencies, remain firmly on the scene.

The most powerful rebellions in half a century may have erupted in the Trump era, but they took aim at a racist fascism that is far older, and all too overlooked by a liberal commentariat fixated on Trumpian "norm busting." As such, the uprisings for Black life and liberation have clarified the scope and shape of contemporary American fascism and anti-fascism in a way never accomplished by preceding debates around Trump, his supporters and policies, or around Antifa and Antifa tactics. I, too, in previous writing on the issue, while insisting that Trump did not *bring* fascism to this country, have failed to emphasize the anti-Blackness at the heart of American fascism's operations: namely, the extension of settler colonialism and racial capitalism.

"As the Black Lives Matter movement has made clear, the threat is not of a 'return of the 1930s' but the ongoing fact of racialized state terror," wrote critical theorist Alberto Toscano in October 2020. "This is the ever-present danger that animates present-day anti-fascist energies in the United States." And as much as a fascist constellation need not bear the name "fascist" to be so (most fascists disavow the label), anti-fascist struggle need not coalesce under the banner of anti-fascism, or Antifa, to be rightly understood as anti-fascist in practice.

Thus, to describe the anti-racist uprisings as also "anti-fascist" is not only accurate—and a way to subvert Trumpian anti-Antifa vitriol—but also recognizes the history of Black radicalism, which has for decades insisted that the US police state be understood as a fascist one. As historian Robyn C. Spencer noted in 2017:

Black history has been marginalized in this burgeoning contemporary discourse about fascism. Analyses of the US as fascist have a long history in the Black intellectual tradition. Black thinkers like Harry Hayward, Claudia Jones, George Jackson and Kuwasi Balagoon used fascism as an analytical framework to understand the rise of segregation in the South after Reconstruction; white populism at the turn of the 19th century; land and labor struggles in the Black Belt South, and the evolution of capitalism in the 1970s.

The commentators who expended considerable energies distinguishing the Trump presidency from a formal fascist regime overlooked not only decades of theorizing on European fascism (as I discuss in the first chapter), but also the historical work of Black radicals in the United States, who rightly insisted on seeing fascism as operative on—and in the very consistency of—US soil, as well as at work through the state's war machine abroad. It was through a lens of anti-fascism that the Black Panthers "sought to make their class and cross-race anti-imperialist politics more explicit," wrote Joshua Bloom and Waldo E. Martin Jr. in *Black against Empire*. The Black Panther Party (BPP), the historians noted, "began widely using *fascism* to describe the U.S. policies of U.S. government" in the late 1960s, a period when the organization was establishing leadership of a revolutionary movement in allegiance with other oppressed communities and liberation fighters around the country and world, from Vietnam to South Africa. In short, fascism became a conceptual hinge that made it possible to unite seemingly distinct movements and diverse constituencies into a common cause opposed to repressive capacities of the American state.

"This is fascism; there's no doubt about it," Angela Davis said in December 1969 at a rally of 4,000 protesters outside Los Angeles City Hall, referring to the brutal police raid on the Panthers' LA headquarters. The raid was the first ever example of a Special Weapons Assault Team (SWAT) attack; cops with M16 rifles, dressed in all-black, military-style uniforms, fired 5,000 rounds at the Panthers' heavily fortified building.

In July of that year, the Panthers organized the United Front against Fascism (UFAF) conference in Oakland, which drew around 5,000 attendees from around the country, with representatives from over 300 organizations. "In addition to the Young Lords, Red Guard, Los Siete de la Raza, Young Patriots, and Third World Liberation Front, attendees included the Peace and Freedom Party, the International Socialist Club, Progressive Labor, Students for a Democratic Society, the Young Socialist Alliance, and various groups within the Women's Liberation Movement," noted Bloom and Martin, "a broad cross-section of the New Left." As might be expected, numerous tense debates arose, including around problems of male supremacy in liberation struggles. Yet there was strong consensus around understanding the US police and carceral state as a locus of fascism. Such a theory differed markedly from a European experience defined by mass fascist parties and the formal suspension of liberal democracy. Nevertheless, it pointed to some unmistakable similarities: authoritarian creep, racialized violence, and an increasingly aggressive posture domestically and abroad in the service of capital.

The conference inaugurated the formation of National Committees to Combat Fascism (NCCFs) in at least eighteen cities: a multiracial network of community groups, organized under the BPP umbrella, that focused on orchestrating local campaigns for community control of police and building legal teams to defend political prisoners. Today's abolitionist fight to defund the police and invest instead in non-carceral systems of community support and economic justice unquestionably belongs to this anti-fascist lineage, yet, as Spencer also pointed out, these historical and conceptual linkages have been lost to popular memory:

In late January 2017, fascism remain[ed] in the top 1 percent of words searched in the US according to Merriam-Webster, leading one news article to opine that "Americans Worried About Fascism." Yet the UFAF's Wikipedia page is two sentences long and does not even acknowledge that the Panthers were the main impetus behind the conference. The NCCFs don't even have a Wikipedia page.

In a 1971 letter from prison that described incarcerated life, revolutionary author George Jackson wrote of the enduring "manifestations of fascism"—"the concrete and steel, the tiny electronic listening device concealed in the vent, the phalanx of goons peeping in"—as well as the intolerable economic realities faced by the Black working class. Jackson was shot dead by prison guards the following year. The incarcerated population at the time of Jackson's execution was around 200,000 people; presently, the country cages well over 2 million people. While Black people make up 13 percent of the general population, they comprise 40 percent of the prison population. It's hardly surprising that the term "fascist" continues to be invoked to describe such a vast archipelago of detention and premature death.

The manifestations of fascism that Jackson and Davis, among others, described have only expanded their reach. Prior to the BPP's decimation by the FBI's merciless COINTELPRO campaign, its efforts to build a "United Front" against fascism expressed what an effective anti-fascist solidarity could look like. It does no justice to that legacy to pretend that we can practice an anti-fascism worthy of the name without prioritizing the fight for police and prison abolition—in short, against the fulcrum of a peculiarly American reaction. "If the growing resistance movement to Trump's fascism is to realize its potential for societal transformation, it must draw from the deep well of Black anti-fascist resistance," Spencer wrote. Three years later, in continuation of that very tradition, the George Floyd rebellions offered the most potent expression of anti-fascist struggle of the Trump era.

Throughout the summer of 2020, the uprisings escalated, de-escalated and re-escalated with shifting loci nationwide— from Atlanta, Philadelphia and Portland, to Louisville, where police had executed Breonna Taylor that March, to Kenosha, Wisconsin, where cops had maimed and paralyzed Jacob Blake when they shot the 29-year-old Black man seven times in the back at close range. Again and again, federal and local law enforcement displayed allegiance with white supremacist militia, who prowled the streets in numerous towns and cities where protests had erupted.

The heavily armed, camo-clad white far-right "patriots" were often indistinguishable from the militarized forces sent in to quash the revolts. Dozens of videos captured instances of cops and federal agents thanking the vigilantes for their presence—the state and civilian fascists in deadly union for whiteness and property against Black life. Government forces were filmed sharing water with and thanking Kyle Rittenhouse, a 17-year-old Trump fanatic who had traveled across state lines to Kenosha. Later that night he shot dead two Black Lives Matter protesters. Leaked Department of Homeland Security memos revealed that its federal agents were later advised to publicly support the right-wing teen and claim that he "took his rifle to the scene of the rioting to help defend small business owners." For federal law enforcement to stand with open white supremacy was by no means unique under Trump; on the contrary, this is the raison d'être of US policing.

As the full weight of the government's law enforcement apparatus bore down on the anti-racist protesters, leaked FBI documents made clear that the agency was well aware that white supremacist groups constituted by far the deadliest threat of extremist violence in the country. Unsurprisingly, however, efforts to crush and weaken the fight for Black lives took priority. During the summer of 2020 there were almost as many federal anti-riot charges as there had been in the previous thirty years combined. That some cities saw vigorous protests last for weeks on end speaks all the more to their tenacity. In Portland, anti-racist standoffs with local police, federal agents and other fascist thugs lasted over one hundred nights.

Five years prior, establishment politics and media had transmogrified the Ferguson and Baltimore rebellions into cries for police reform—which they were not. But the fires of 2020 largely resisted such reduction, despite ample liberal efforts. The demand from the streets to abolish the police—at the very least to defund them—would not be contained, even as the summer's great wave of riotous protest calmed.

The uprisings carried forward the legacy of anti-racist anti-fascism rooted not in twentieth-century Europe, but in the Black radical tradition that has long insisted that racist fascism coexists within, rather than in antagonism to, US liberal democracy. Less interested in comparing an American president to Hitler or Mussolini, this capacious anti-fascism recognizes the continuity from slavery and colonial oppression, through the overthrow of Reconstruction and the establishment of Jim Crow rule, to the fascistic operations of carcerality to which Black life is subjugated to this day. There is a history of mutual enrichment between abolitionist Black anti-fascism and the forebears of contemporary Antifa; indeed, the genealogies are not *entirely* distinct. But, as the uprisings of multiracial rebels exemplified, in the legacy of the Panthers and the long Black radical tradition, the struggle against American fascism is, has always been, and necessarily will be forged in the fight for Black liberation.

Making Felons

"It's crazy, a few windows got smashed," twenty-three-year-old Olivia Alsip said, two months after her arrest on felony riot charges. "Why are 214 people looking at ten years in prison?"

Alsip knew only one other person at the protest march on the day of her arrest. The political science graduate student from the University of Chicago had met her partner in November, when the two had joined the camps at Standing Rock opposing the Dakota Access Pipeline. When they heard about calls to protest Donald J. Trump's inauguration under the banner "Disrupt J20," on January 20 in DC, they felt they had to be there. "I identify as an anarchist, and I've been an activist for women's and queer rights since the eighth grade," Alsip told me over the phone from Chicago.

Alsip was among 214 defendants facing felony riot charges, up to a decade in prison and a $25,000 fine for their participation in the anti-capitalist, anti-fascist march, which ended with a mass arrest on the morning of Inauguration Day 2017. As far as the student understood, the evidence against her amounted to little more than proof of her presence at the unruly protest, as indicated by her arrest. Like the vast majority of her codefendants, Alsip didn't break or throw anything. Yet, until the last of the charges against the Disrupt J20 defendants were dismissed in July 2018, she would live in shock over the steep price she and her fellow protesters might have to pay as the new administration and police forces set the tone for how they would deal with the spike in organized dissent.

Anarchists and anti-fascist activists across the country have responded to Trump's ascendancy, and particularly the attendant emboldening of white supremacists, with confrontational protest. Rivers of digital ink were spilled approving and denouncing the meme-friendly punch delivered to neo-Nazi Richard Spencer, as well as the militant demonstrations that prevented far-right troll Milo Yiannopoulos from waxing hateful at UC Berkeley (see chapter 1). But while scattered vandalism and punching (of neo-Nazis) were deemed headline-grabbing militancy, the media relegated the most extreme incidents involving anarchists and anti-fascists—namely, their subsequent treatment by the state—to footnotes.

A *New York Times* article about anarchist protests, published two weeks after the 2017 inauguration, accorded just half a sentence to the fact that a Yiannopoulos supporter in Seattle shot and seriously injured an anti-fascist activist. Fifteen paragraphs down, a mere mention was given to the mass arrest of the 200-plus anti-fascist protesters on Inauguration Day. The fact that these arrestees went on to face felony riot charges would go unmentioned by the *Times*—blanket charges, which carried a heft unheard of in recent decades of protest history.

"In my over thirty years of practicing law, I've never seen anything like this," said veteran DC attorney Mark Goldstone, of the charges. Goldstone, who has defended dozens of activist cases and represented six of the J20 defendants, called the charges "unprecedented territory."

Dragnet arrests at protests are nothing new—recall the fall 2011 arrest of over 700 Occupy protesters on the Brooklyn Bridge. Nor is the leveling of serious criminal charges to demonstrators accused of property damage: with a legal logic seemingly opposite to that in the J20 cases, just one man was blamed for the $50,000 of property damage wrought during the 2009 Pittsburgh G20 Summit; he was convicted of felony criminal mischief and three misdemeanors. But the charge of felony riot is in itself rare, let alone when applied to over 200 people.

The charges all stemmed from a single mass arrest of protesters who had taken part in the Disrupt J20 march. It was a typical "black bloc" march, in which protesters mask their faces and wear all black. More than 500 participants gathered some two miles north of the inaugural parade route and surged southward, marching, chanting, and crowding the streets as an aesthetically united force. Whether illegal activity occurred in the context of the march is not in question. By the time the DC Metropolitan Police moved in with pepper spray and flash-bang grenades, a number of march participants were smashing windows—of banks, of chain restaurants, of a limo. Some pulled trash cans into the street, some set off handheld fireworks, and one cop was hit by a rock. Police filings claim that protesters damaged more than $100,000 worth of property that day (a figure that includes destruction caused after the mass arrest).

But no one—neither the police nor the government— suggested that most, or even many, of the arrestees directly engaged in property destruction or violence. Nonetheless, the police department and the government maintained not only that a dragnet arrest was appropriate, but that the police had probable cause to believe that each and every one of the more than 200 arrestees had "willfully incited or urged others to engage in the riot." On this point, the law is precise: even in the case of an alleged riot, the police must have probable cause to arrest each and every individual.

"All the police officers were outstanding in the judgment that we used," Metropolitan Police Department Chief Peter Newsham said the day after the inauguration. "I couldn't be more proud of the way this department responded." Mayor Muriel Bowser tweeted her support for "our officers as they handled crowds." In fact, it was precisely police judgment that problematized these riot charges.

The original arrestees included a handful of professional journalists, medics and legal observers, most of whom would have their charges dropped over the subsequent days and weeks. Of the remaining 214 arrestees, a handful of individuals also faced property damage charges, having been allegedly identified smashing windows. One man, Alsip's partner, was charged with felony assault on a police officer for allegedly throwing the rock that struck a cop; he was identified by his shoes.

As pretrial court proceedings entered the discovery phase, the prosecution's position became clear: the evidence against numerous defendants amounted to no more than video footage of their continued presence in the march and their choice of black bloc attire. If the mass arrest was imprecise enough to sweep up journalists and legal observers, how can it be maintained that the police had probable cause to arrest every single other protester for riot and incitement? If continued presence, proximity and black garb are sufficient to meet the necessary legal standard of individuated probable cause for arrest and prosecution under these charges, the DC police and the government have, from day one of Trump's presidency, lowered the standard for what it takes to turn a protester into a felon.

Mara Verheyden-Hilliard, the executive director of the Partnership for Civil Justice Fund, a legal organization that has long fought civil and human rights cases, expressed concern about police employment of dragnet mass arrests without particularized probable cause. She said that arrests "simply based on proximity or shared political views at a march" set a troubling precedent for all protests—not just for anarchist marches. She explained that "it means at any demonstration," if a participant or a provocateur commits an illegal act, then "the entire demonstration can be subject to indiscriminate force and large groups of people can be suddenly arrested without notice or opportunity to disperse, and face life-altering charges."

Mass arrests, let alone those carrying felony charges, have been rare in DC since 2002, when then–assistant police chief Peter Newsham (a position made permanent in February 2017) ordered the arrest of around 400 people during an anti–World Bank / anti-IMF demonstration in Pershing Park. The dragnet arrest included both peaceful protesters and bystanders walking to work, leading to years of litigation and an $8.25 million settlement on the part of the Justice Department and Department of the Interior. It also led to the establishment of policies and statutes governing protest policing and defending First Amendment activity in the capital. "From the first day of the Trump administration, Newsham and the police department have really stepped back in time," said Verheyden-Hilliard.

I had joined the march at its genesis at Logan Circle, as participants tightened black bandanas around their faces and gathered in formation behind block-wide banners. I heard glass crack around us as we snaked through the city's wide boulevards, and some protesters peeled from formation to take a rock or a stick to a window. Chants common to contemporary US protest boomed louder than any breaking glass: "*No Trump, no KKK, no fascist USA!*" At no point did the police move in to grab individuals as they destroyed property, but after minutes that felt longer than they lasted, cops charged the group en masse.

After one group of protesters broke through a police line on the intersection of L and Twelfth Streets, cops penned in the remaining crowd of 230 and held them there for more than four hours before taking them into holding. In the chaos of charging police, wafting pepper spray, and scrambling protesters, I had detached from the crowd just half a block before the cops closed in. "When the police kettled us [corralled them into a net], they pushed us all into one big writhing mass with not enough room to stand," Alsip recalled. "When they stepped back, people were screaming and crying because they had just been maced or hit."

The government claimed that First Amendment protections didn't apply in the J20 cases, because property damage began "from the jump" (i.e., immediately). Their indictment states that protesters "did not exercise multiple opportunities to leave the Black Bloc," and that they cheered and chanted "Fuck it up," "Fuck capitalism" and "Whose streets?" (slogans that have peppered most every protest I've attended, from Occupy to environmental marches to Black Lives Matter).

According to Verheyden-Hilliard, such a claim goes against fifty years of cases in which property damage or violence occurs during First Amendment activity. "The glue that holds this group together is First Amendment activity," she said. "The line that violence began 'from the jump' distracts from the fact that the police acted unlawfully, as we can see from the fact that the government is trying to extricate particularized probable cause after the fact."

At a pretrial status hearing I attended in March at the high modernist DC Superior Court building, Assistant United States Attorney Jennifer Kerkhoff told the court that the government had collected more than 600 hours of video footage and data pulled from more than one hundred cell phones taken from the arrestees. She said that each defendant would be shown individuated evidence of their participation in the riot and its incitement. But during a late-March conference call with fifteen other lawyers representing J20 clients, Mark Goldstone learned that for a number of defendants this alleged evidence amounted to no more than, as he put it, "Here's your client at the beginning of the march, wearing black clothes and goggles, your client could have left but did not, and here is your client at the end, in the police kettle." "The scary thing about it," said Goldstone, "is that defendants who want to test that theory have to be willing to face a jury, who could uphold the government's line." It's not hard to demonize a masked protester.

As such, while civil liberties groups and legal support groups stress police misconduct and prosecutorial overreach, the pressure for defendants to plead out in such cases is high. And where pleas are extracted from defendants, the ability to bring civil litigation against the police department is significantly diminished—if not foreclosed. In their use of lengthy prison sentences to attempt to extract pleas out of court, the J20 cases recapitulated a predicament all too typical of the judicial process in this country.

Early in the court proceedings, in spring 2017, an eighteen-year-old man pleaded guilty to one count of misdemeanor rioting or inciting to riot, a suspended 180-day sentence, one year of supervised probation, a $500 fine, and fifty hours of community service. Because he was under twenty-three years of age, the defendant was charged under the Youth Act, which allows for a young person who "will derive benefit" to get special treatment under the law. This did not apply to most every other arrestee, most of whom were between twenty-five and forty. "The plea deal that was accepted by one defendant was both a bad deal and irrelevant to everyone else's cases," the Dead City Legal Posse, a DC volunteer legal support group set up to assist the J20 cases, wrote in a statement.

The support group does not offer legal advice, but it commented on perhaps the most salient information to come from the plea. "After the plea deal was accepted, the prosecutor is required to say what the government 'would have been able to prove,'" the collective noted. According to the group, the government was able to show only the following: that the defendant joined a black bloc with 200 other people; marched with the black bloc for thirty minutes; had multiple opportunities to leave and did not; wore black clothes and goggles; and in the words of the prosecutor, "knew or reasonably should have known that the black bloc was causing destruction" and

63

that "the actions of the black bloc caused and constituted a riot."

This, the statement noted, was "literally all they had on him." As the cases against more and more defendants came to rest on the same scant evidence, it didn't take a defender of black bloc tactics to see a dangerous legal precedent quietly crystallizing; ten years in prison would be an extreme punishment for breaking windows. However, the J20 cases were not an occasion to debate the moral (or tactical) merits and flaws of political property damage. How could they have been? Most J20 defendants broke nothing at all.

Of the dozens of New York activists I know who traveled to DC to join the J20 protests and the vast but placid Women's March the following day, three were arrested in the kettle. In the week that followed the J20 arrests, the names and personal information—including some addresses of arrestees—were made public by far-right site GotNews, and the New Yorkers I spoke to claimed to have received numerous online threats.

One twenty-nine-year-old Brooklyn-based protester told me that this sort of harassment highlights one impetus for deploying black bloc tactics in the first place—tactics that have grave implications for less seasoned dissenters. "Clearly, it was in the best interest of everyone present for the anti-fascist march on the day of my arrest to conceal their identities," he said, "because in the current climate in which we exist, the danger is very real."

But, in a moment when the shock of felony charges and the arduousness of a lengthy legal process still weighed on the defendant, he also told me he was surprised and heartened by the supportive attitude toward the black bloc of some more mainstream anti-Trump protesters. He said that following his release from jail on January 21, he went with some friends to DC institution Ben's Chili Bowl. "We found quite a few pink pussy hat–wearing Women's March attendees inside," he said. He asked the women what they felt about the Richard Spencer punch and the J20 protests, expecting that they might repeat historical denunciations of "bad protesters." "To my surprise," he told me, the women said that they wished they could have punched Spencer themselves. "The women thanked me for being in DC that weekend and for everything that took place on the twentieth."

Government actions like the J20 mass arrest could make the tired "good protester / bad protester" narrative obsolete—if presence, proximity and chanting are sufficient to constitute a "bad protester." And while radical leftists would collapse this dichotomy by banishing the "bad protester" label, the state seems keen to erase the concept of "good" protest. During the J20 defendants' preliminary hearings in February 2017, Republican lawmakers in at least eighteen states introduced legislation to increase the severity of charges for traditionally nonviolent protest tactics, such as blocking highways.

Trump's government has proven its willingness to set what Goldstone called "a monstrous trap" for protesters, by leveraging high risk trials against paper-thin cases.

"It definitely hits in waves," Alsip told me. "I'm nervous. I try to think that even if I do go to prison, I would remain committed, and politically active. But," she paused, "I just can't believe that my thoughts have to go there. And that we're all facing this." Another pause. "A few broken windows."

Addendum: *In the months that followed this essay's original publication in spring 2017, the infirmity of the government's case was borne out. The first group of defendants to go to trial were acquitted by a jury in December 2017. Soon after, the government dismissed charges against 129 more defendants, claiming that it wished to focus the prosecution on the perpetrators of the most serious vandalism. The following May, a DC Superior Court judge sanctioned prosecutors for failing to disclose potentially exculpatory evidence to the defense before trial. The government was also found to have submitted to evidence videos edited to exclude evidence favorable to the defense; the videos were made by right-wing provocateurs Project Veritas. The second trial ended with one defendant acquitted and a deadlocked jury (and so a mistrial) for three other defendants. The prosecutors dismissed charges against the remaining thirty-nine defendants in July 2018. A number of defendants plan to file complaints against the prosecutors for their misconduct; the ACLU has filed suit against the Metropolitan Police Department for its behavior during the protest.*

Freedom for Herman Bell

This piece was drafted in 2017, intended for publication in The Nation *magazine. At the time, former Black Panther Herman Bell was awaiting his eighth parole hearing, after over four decades in prison. Bell bore a mark of Cain in the distorted moral universe of the American criminal legal system: he was a Black radical convicted of killing two cops. I was writing to call for his long-overdue freedom. But I pulled the piece from publication at the last minute; fears were mounting that media attention could sour the parole board against Bell and further incite the fanatical police unions fighting to keep him behind bars until his death. I wrote the piece for Bell; I pulled it from print for him, too.*

I publish a version here to honor those elders who struggle for Black liberation and remain caged. Free Them All. And for my friend Herman, an inspiration.

December 2017

When seated, Herman Bell looked sturdy. He rested his strong forearms on the small metal table, his broad shoulders relaxed forward. His pronounced cheekbones, pursed smile and neat moustache looked almost unchanged from photographs taken over forty years ago, when he was last free. Everything now was just a little greyer.

It was only when he stood up to say goodbye that I saw the limp in the then-69-year-old's step, as he walked back to his cell in New York's maximum security Shawangunk Correctional Facility.

"How do you get your head around being seventy in prison?" Bell had asked, earlier that day—more to himself than me—as we sat in a designated empty room with towering grey walls, scant daylight and an inmate-painted mural of orange skies and cherubs. A guard sat in the corner, looking at the floor. Bell's seventieth birthday is on January 14; one month later he will go before the parole board for the eighth time. "The notion that some people never get out—how do you wrap your mind around that?" he asked.

Bell's institutional record over his forty-four incarcerated years has been exemplary. He's earned degrees, launched educational programs, mentored fellow inmates, and maintained close friends, a loving marriage and a family, as well as broad public support. Beyond prison walls, he's organized community gardening projects and homeless youth outreach initiatives, continuing the legacy of the Black Panther Party's Survival Programs. "He has the respect not only of other inmates," his attorney, Robert Boyle, told me, "but of prison staff, too." The New York State Department of Corrections and Community Supervision (DOCCS) has assigned him the lowest risk score in its determinations about his likelihood of recidivism. Despite all this, Bell has been denied parole seven times—every two years since his first eligibility in 2004.

Bell's risk score was no higher in his prior parole applications, but the board has nonetheless consistently ruled, contra the corrections department's own metrics of risk, against his release. The board's decision takes the same form every time: "There is a reasonable probability that he would not live and remain at liberty without again violating the law and that release would be incompatible with the welfare of society and would so deprecate the serious nature of the crime as to undermine respect for the law."

"I can't see the sense of keeping me in this place," said Bell with a shrug. He might not see the sense, but he knows the reason.

By the perverse, racist logic of American carcerality, Bell had been deemed irredeemable. In 1973, while active in the Black Panther Party (BPP), he was convicted, along with co-defendants Jalil Abdul Muntaqim and Albert "Nuh" Washington, of murdering NYPD officers Joseph Piagentini and Waverly Jones in a 1971 shooting in Harlem. He was sentenced to twenty-five years to life.

Bell is one of fifteen former Panthers still incarcerated in the United States, most of whom were also convicted of murdering law enforcement officers in the 1960s and '70s, a time when the government targeted Black liberation fighters with ferocity. These prisoners are aging, and aging in prison means getting old fast: long-term incarceration is said to add ten years to a person's physical age. Since 2000, eight former BPP members have died while incarcerated, all aged between thirty-nine and seventy-one; most were in their fifties and sixties. Washington, Bell's co-defendant, died in 2000 of liver cancer, aged sixty-four.

All of the living imprisoned former Panthers are now over sixty-five, which, according to a 2012 American Civil Liberties Union report based on DOCCS statistics, puts them in an age bracket with a less than 4 percent recidivism rate. In New York, 0.4 percent of individuals convicted of murder who are then released on parole ever return to prison on a new offense.

Every prisoner is, in a sense, a political prisoner: who can be deemed criminal and caged as such are decisions drenched in politics. But the former BPP members aging and dying behind bars are political prisoners in an absolute sense: the *homo sacer*—life under total control of the state, excluded with ostensible permanence from society, designated worth neither saving nor killing.

As Laura Whitehorn, an organizer with the project Release Aging People in Prison (RAPP), a longtime friend of Bell and a former political prisoner herself, explains, the irony therein is breathtaking: "Of all the political prisoners who have been released in recent decades, not one has gone back to prison. Not one."

At the time of writing, no Black Panther convicted of murdering a police officer has ever been freed.

Bell's eighth parole hearing comes at a moment of historical resonance with the era of his murder conviction. Under President Donald Trump and the emboldened racism of our time, the US government is constructing a fulcrum according to which the claim that Black lives matter is an assertion of an extremist identitarian position.

An FBI report leaked in October 2017 warned of a mythic threat: "BIE," that is, "Black identity extremists." The memo connects today's phantom "Black identity extremism" to "violence" that "peaked in the 1960s and 1970s." The document all but endorsed the strategy of the FBI under J. Edgar Hoover and its notorious and illegal COINTELPRO activities, which took aggressive aim at social justice movements, particularly the struggle for Black liberation. The objective, in Hoover's words, was to "disrupt, misdirect, discredit or otherwise neutralize" movement groups by any means necessary. In 1975, the Senate's Church Committee revealed the full extent of the program: infiltration, harassment, surveillance, assassination and a glut of wrongful imprisonment. Former Panthers continued to be targeted for decades after COINTELPRO was shuttered; indeed, the program's tactics were never retired. The fervor with which police unions and powerful politicians fight to keep aging Panthers in prison until their dying day is congruous with contemporary efforts to demonize Black struggle.

Government and police misconduct in the investigations of the BPP are case studies in how structural racism and political targeting can overwhelm due process, and they should not be expunged from memory. Yet, the time for relitigating Bell's case has long passed. He takes full responsibility for the bloodshed and expresses "great sorrow" for the lives lost at that time.

Five men, including Bell, were tried for the ambush-style murders of officers Piagentini and Jones. Their first trial ended in a hung jury; the second saw charges dropped against two defendants for lack of evidence. In the second trial, as Bell's defense team argued in appeals, witness statements had been coerced through torture and imprisonment, not one eye witness had identified Bell as the shooter, and post-conviction revelations about FBI involvement with the NYPD investigations had raised concerns that the prosecution withheld exculpatory ballistics and forensic evidence. But the so-called New York Three exhausted their appeals options without avail, which, by the grim vagaries of the procedural system, meant justice has been served.

"I do think about it," Bell said of his lengthy trials and appeals process, "but I want to move on."

By any measure, even the state's own, Bell has served his time and poses no risk to society. According to the parole board's rules, this should be the principle guiding whether he is granted release. Even the son of one of the victims, Waverly Jones Jr., has advocated for Bell's freedom for many years. "I feel that Herman Bell and Anthony Bottom were both victims as well of a much larger scheme which got them incarcerated to this day," Jones Jr., who *The Nation* was unable to locate for comment, wrote in his statement to the parole board in 2004. "Their spirit is still eager to do good, and I just pray that the Parole Board will look at the context and the time and send a message to me of healing."

But Jones Jr.'s support is countered fiercely by the surviving family of Officer Piagentini. His widow, Diane, has spoken publicly in advance of both Bell and his co-defendent's previous parole hearings, urging that they never be freed. At a filmed press conference hosted in 2014 by the belligerent New York City Patrolmen's Benevolent Association (NYCPBA), for example, the diminutive Piagentini repeated the painful story of losing her husband. On the May night that the officers were gunned down from behind, she waited for her husband with a dinner of pasta e fagioli on the stove, their young daughters tucked in bed. He never came home, and she believes that Bell and his co-defendant should "never be paroled."

The political weight of the NYCPBA's promulgation of this same message is no small factor in Bell's continued imprisonment.

Powerful police unions treat the continued incarceration of prisoners like Bell as a moral crusade. An entire page on the NYCPBA website is entitled "Keep Cop-Killers In Jail." It encourages visitors to click through and send pre-written, automated letters to state officials objecting to parole for so-called cop-killers. You can pick a specific "cop-killer," or your letter can simply oppose the notion that anyone convicted of murdering a cop should ever see the light of day again.

In advance of Bell's previous parole hearings, the NYCPBA has given stern press conferences and rallied the support of powerful politicians, including former mayor Michael Bloomberg, to advocate against the aging prisoner's parole.

NYCPBA president Patrick Lynch's comment on Bell's upcoming hearing was not so much a statement as it was a fire-and-brimstone sermon. "The evil that manifested itself in the planned, brutal assassinations of police officers Joseph Piagentini and Waverly Jones can never be rehabilitated," he wrote via email. "That evil goes to the very core of a person's existence and while years in prison may suppress or disguise it, that evil is still there and it should never be free to endanger our streets again."

Lynch is a notorious and blustering defender of some of the most egregious incidences of police violence and impunity, including the 2014 choking death of Eric Garner and the 2004 shooting of unarmed teen Timothy Stansbury Jr.; he has stood in staunch opposition to even the suggestion of police reform. His Old Testament claims about Bell speak not only to a disregard for the putative principles of parole, but also to rabid ideological commitment to the unparalleled mattering of Blue Lives.

Yet, despite the will of the police union, the parole board's own regulations demand that "risks and needs assessments" are given precedence. In 2016, five new parole commissioners were nominated by Governor Andrew Cuomo and approved by the state senate. "They got rid of some of the worst commissioners," Whitehorn tells me. A number of the new appointees have a history in public health and family services, rather than the law enforcement careers typical of parole commissioners.

A spokesperson from the New York State DOCCS explains that concerted efforts have been made to increase "geographic, racial and professional diversity" on the board. He notes that when board chairwoman Tina Stanford was appointed in 2013 (the second African American woman to hold that position), "there were two African American females on the board, one African American male, and two Hispanic females. Currently, there are sixteen members including two African American males, three African American females, and two Hispanic females." Whether such a demographic shift in the composition of the board leads to an improvement in the gaping racial disparities in release rates, however, only time will tell.

With an aging and ailing prison population that the state can scarcely afford to house, parole commissioners who deny parole applications for low risk, elderly prisoners shoot their own departments in the foot. But application denial is often the standard: as writer Victoria Law reported on New York State parole decisions in the *Village Voice*, "Despite the state's own findings that people over age 65 were least likely to commit new crimes, of the thirty-three applicants aged sixty or older, only nine were released."

Meanwhile, a 2016 *New York Times* investigation found consistent racial disparities in the state parole system.

Analyzing decisions from 2013, the report found that fewer than one in six Black or Latino men was released at his first hearing, compared with one in four white men. It found that the board, overwhelmingly white at the time, treated parole hearings like a fast-paced assembly line.

Whitehorn stresses the absurdity of continuing to incarcerate long-term, elderly prisoners who have served their minimum sentences and have been deemed to pose no threat to society. "Are we talking about hysteria or public health?"

RAPP, along with other prisoner advocacy organizations in New York, is thus pushing the state assembly to pass legislation for presumptive parole for elders. They're advocating a bill that would direct the board to give presumption of parole to people over fifty-five or who have served ten or fifteen years unless there is current evidence that they would present a danger to others. Current law on presumptive release excludes those convicted of violent crimes, but existing guidelines for parole decisions already state that determinations of the prisoner's risks and chances of recidivism should be primary in parole decisions. In October 2017, parole board administrators brought in new regulations in an attempt to instantiate what should have long been standard practice: basing parole decisions on a system of evaluating the inmate's risk to the public instead of emphasizing the nature of the crime that led to their incarceration.

"A presumptive parole bill would not be needed if the board followed the principles already in their regulations—focus[ing] on risk and needs assessments, which show that Herman and other long termers pose little if any risk to public safety," Whitehorn explains. "But since the board keeps reflecting police thinking and relying on the person's original crime to keep them locked up, we need something like this bill to make them do what they should."

Such "police thinking" treats situations like Bell's as the limit cases for any universal application of presumptive parole for elders. In response to a question about the union's views on presumptive parole regulation, the NYCPBA was unwavering. As a spokesperson told me, "Anyone convicted of killing a police officer should never be released on parole, regardless of age."

Bell has what carceral parlance names "a reintegration plan." He has job offers and a place to live in California with his wife of twenty-seven years, Nancy Jacot-Bell. There's enough money to live on. He knows if he's released, he has family members and loved ones waiting to embrace him. But he's dreaming, too, of his first free hours alone.

"I would take a bus from the joint to the city," he told me. The hour-and-a-half journey parallels the Hudson River's southward wind. When we met in November, the upstate mountains were rich with the browns, reds and burnt sienna of the late-autumn leaves. The cell bars inside Shawangunk, where you can't see the trees, are painted crimson. "I would go to the city, and watch out the window as the skyline appears," said Bell, who went to prison the very year that the construction of the Twin Towers was completed. "But then I'd need someone to pick me up," he said, "because I'd be totally lost."

"I just really want to go for a walk with him, and look up at the sky and see no barbed wire behind his head," his wife told me. Jacot-Bell met her husband in 1974 over the phone; she was working as a legal secretary and believed in the principles of the Black Panther Party. "I liked what they had to say," she told me. They became very good friends, and their friendship developed into romance and lifelong partnership. "I couldn't ask for a better companion," said Bell of his wife.

But time is on the side of those parties who would see the likes of Bell die behind bars. He is already older than a number of his former Panther counterparts who have met such a fate.

The most recent death of a former BPP member in prison came in April 2016, when Abdul Majid died at Five Points Correctional Facility in upstate New York, aged sixty-five. Also convicted of killing a cop, he was sentenced to twenty-five years to life in 1986 for the murder of Officer John Scarangella and the attempted murder of Officer Richard Rainey in 1981 (an incident on the tail end of active Black Panther activity). Majid was one month away from his first parole hearing when he died of gallbladder inflammation—an ailment that is almost never serious, let alone fatal, when treated correctly.

The last time I saw Majid, a few months prior to his death, his eyes welled up behind crooked, wire frame glasses. Looking to the ceiling and the walls, he told me his greatest fear: "rotting away in this place."

Majid maintained his innocence until his death. "I'm not going to say I did something that I didn't do," Majid told me as we sat in a small glass cubicle, interrupted every few minutes by the crackle and drone of orders transmitted over cell block speakers.

As Majid's attorney and my longtime friend Moira Meltzer-Cohen said, "There are so many things that cast doubt on the investigation and the proceedings." Throw a dart at the case records and transcripts and you'll hit a reason to doubt, if not entirely dismiss the legal proceedings and their conclusion.

Over five years, including two mistrials, the prosecution built a house-of-cards case against the men based on shaky circumstantial evidence from coerced, inconsistent and racist witnesses, some of whom were even hypnotized. The jury that convicted him was nearly all white and elderly. The three Black jurors selected were all over retirement age, and all had relatives in or connections to law enforcement.

At the time of Majid's death, Meltzer-Cohen had sent out Freedom of Information Act requests to the NYPD, having found inconsistencies in early police reports on the case. She was also preparing Majid for his first parole hearing. "We had a beautiful parole packet ready," the attorney said.

When she learned of his death, having called the prison to inquire about her client after a few rare weeks of not hearing from him, she told me she almost fell over. "I lost my balance entirely," she said. "He had been in fine health. In my view, it was something that could have been treated and it was not treated." Having converted to Islam in prison, Majid had stipulated that his body should not be autopsied. According to the Onondaga County Medical Examiner's office, he died of "natural causes."

Meltzer-Cohen calls the loss of Majid behind bars "one of the great tragedies" observed in her life. Attempts to posthumously overturn the former Panther's conviction have died with him. "The point," said his friend and lawyer, "was his freedom."

Responding to his death in the *New York Daily News*, the NYCPBA's Lynch said, "The city of New York and this earth is a far better place without the likes of Laborde and his band of blood thirsty domestic terrorists."

"What happened to Majid," Bell said of his fellow Panther's passing, "shouldn't have happened." But the 70-year-old is all too aware of the vulnerability of elderly life behind bars. Just last September, half a dozen guards at Great Meadow Correctional Facility in Comstock, New York, beat him bloody and broke two of his ribs. He thought he was going to die.

Both his wife and his daughter-in-law, kihana miraya ross— the mother of two of his granddaughters—said the assault has been one of the hardest things to watch Bell endure. "I think about it every day," said ross, an assistant professor of African American studies at Northwestern University.

"When I'm cutting onions, and my eyes are stinging and watering, I think about what it must have been like to be maced at close range. When I have a headache, I think about what it must have been like to be hit and kicked while a guard repeatedly slams your head into the concrete," she said, adding, "And then to have to stay in a system that effectively committed attempted murder with impunity, is just—there are no words for such things."

Following the incident (which is, according to DOCCS, under active and ongoing investigation) attempts to charge the elderly prisoner with assault fell flat and were dropped within weeks. This is almost unheard of—95 percent of prisoners charged with assaulting a guard are convicted, and in Bell's case there were no witnesses but the guards themselves.

Nonetheless, Bell awaits his February parole hearing, relocated to Shawangunk, with a body on the mend and a gleaming disciplinary record intact.

A post on Bell's support website called his recent beating "a stark reminder that, while Herman poses no danger to society, his continued imprisonment as an elder subjects him to extreme danger." Bell himself is less somber. "Life goes on; I'm still here," he told me. Majid was always courageous, too.

Addendum: At Bell's eighth hearing, in March 2018, the parole board granted him release. The police union immediately filed suit to block the decision, delaying his release until late April. In the weeks during which his long-overdue freedom was further postponed, his wife Nancy passed away. They had no time together beyond the prison walls.

While for three years the police union has exhausted every avenue attempting to re-imprison him, Bell has been rebuilding his life in Brooklyn. "When I got out, I found that preparing for a thing and experiencing it are quite different. Then and now I find that I have to relearn much of what I once knew and took for granted," he told me recently. "A striking thing, among so many, was the cost of a loaf of bread, a dozen eggs, a gallon of milk; and I must include perfecting a MetroCard 'swipe' and how to place it in the change slot when getting on a city bus."

To an outside observer, Bell makes the adjustment look easy. He visits friends, works with families of the still-incarcerated, takes trips to the beach, and texts with a surfeit of emojis. He listens to Jazz and R & B, reads history and sci-fi, and visits museums and parks; he enjoys, he says, an occasional ride on the Staten Island Ferry, "believe it or not." He got his driver's license again within months, and was back on a bike even sooner. He says my inability to ride a bike is unacceptable; I've promised to let him teach me, and I'd trust almost no one else to do it. The first time I saw Bell outside of prison, he looked ten years younger, in jeans and now-trademark sunglasses, laid-back and cracking jokes. Before the pandemic hit, we were trying to learn to cook together in my apartment in Bedford-Stuyvesant, from recipes my mother would email over from London—our Thai curry is pretty damn good. Herman Bell can, as very few people can, be accurately described as cool.

To those who took to the streets for Black liberation, joining the legacy Bell helped build, he says "Keep at it!" His desire for justice is unwavering. "I would love to witness a radical turn in our society toward social justice, defunding where appropriate, prison abolition, universal health care, free education, equitable taxation, Black reparations," he told me.

In September 2020, Bell's co-defendant, Jalil Muntaqim, was also granted parole after nearly half a century behind bars.

Still Fighting at Standing Rock

Rattler sat on the sofa scrolling through his phone. It was a drizzling, cold spring day in Bismarck, North Dakota, but he wasn't going outside much anyway. A great mountain of a man with thick black hair to his waist and a disarming gentleness, Rattler made the objects around him look small. The sofa on which he sat, the phone he held, the homey living room where we met—the whole city of Bismarck seemed too small for Rattler. But his bail conditions and an ankle monitor confined him to the area for over half a year as he awaited trial.

He put the phone down. "I was looking for a quote," he said, "about how the people have the right to overthrow the government if it abuses its power. Who said that?"

Sandra Freeman, Rattler's attorney, sat with him on the sofa. She ventured that the line he was seeking might be from the Declaration of Independence. Rattler didn't return to his phone to check. If he had, he may have noticed that Jefferson's founding document—that vaunted proclamation of America and its values—described the land's native peoples, his ancestors, as "merciless Indian savages."

Rattler, forty-five, legal name Michael Markus, is one of six native activists who faced near-unprecedented federal charges related to the Standing Rock protest camps against the Dakota Access Pipeline (DAPL). The federal cases sat alongside hundreds and hundreds brought by state prosecutors, stemming from vast numbers of arrests made over the six months that the camps stood. At its height, the protest drew as many as 15,000 participants from around the world and, for a short time, the dilettantish gaze of the mainstream media. The authorities razed the last major holdouts of the camps on February 23, 2017, by which point numbers had dwindled as blizzard conditions pummeled the prairie lands. The camera crews packed up, and most of the country went back to focusing on Trump.

But for Rattler, his federal codefendants, the many hundreds of arrestees facing state charges, and their lawyers, the fight on the ground in North Dakota was far from over. They faced a terrain as brutal and unforgiving as any winter on the Standing Rock Reservation: a small-town court system in conservative rural counties that had no experience of anything nearing this scale or political valence.

The fate of the DAPL standoff resided not only in judicial decisions about the flow of oil. Those who stood on the front lines for clean water, for indigenous struggle, for their ancestors and for our future, were brought to alleged justice in an area with doubtful prospects for anything resembling an impartial jury. North Dakota prosecutor Ladd Erickson told me over the phone that prior to the Standing Rock cases, the only mass arrest incidents that these local counties had dealt with involved breaking up graduation parties of drunk high schoolers. And while thousands flocked to the protest camps, only a few dozen lawyers and supporters remained and returned to continue the arduous and overwhelming task of defending these cases, in an area where towns consist of interconnected parking lots, strip mall restaurants and boxy houses, surrounded by unending sightlines of rolling grassland. When I went to North Dakota in April 2017, 140 defendants still didn't even have legal representation.

"The reality is that the frontlines are in the courthouse now," said Freeman, a former public defender who moved from Colorado to live in North Dakota full time to fight the DAPL arrest cases. She is one among a small cadre of lawyers and legal support workers who put their normal lives on hold in order to seek justice for water protectors facing trial in the conservative, rural Midwest. "The celebration and camaraderie of the camp—that's gone," she said, "but we're left to stand with people going into the gauntlet, facing incarceration for being who they are."

The Dakota Access Pipeline has since been fully built, following President Donald Trump's January 2017 order to expedite its completion, reversing President Obama's block on the project. In June, crude oil began pumping from North Dakota's Bakken Formation to Illinois, under the Mississippi river and through sacred Lakota land and burial sites. In November 2017, the pipeline spilled over 210,000 gallons over South Dakota farmland. A major spill risks contaminating the main water source of the Standing Rock Sioux and 17 million people who live downstream. The summer prior to the spill, a federal judge ruled that the Army Corps of Engineers, responsible for approving the pipeline's route and completion, had not adequately considered the impacts of a spill into the Missouri River. The decision was a partial victory for the Standing Rock Sioux Tribe, but it was still too little, too late, and oil continues to flow through the DAPL. From February 2017, anti-pipeline activists began to take their fight from North Dakota to new camps across the United States, opposing pipeline construction and fracking operations from Nebraska and Iowa, to Texas, Louisiana and Florida, to Pennsylvania, New Jersey, and Massachusetts.

On the first night I spoke to Sandra Freeman in the dingy apartment rented by her legal collective in Mandan—the small town in which most of the hundreds of state cases were tried—she pulled out a dog-eared map of the area. On it were the lines of the Fort Laramie treaties, which drew up the Great Sioux Reservation in 1851 and 1868. And next to it, Freeman roughly sketched how the land today—the site of the pipeline standoff—is broken up into federal, private and reservation property. "The history of exploitation and extraction cannot be disconnected from what's happening here," she said.

The unbroken American history of native oppression is not lost on Rattler, a marine veteran, truck driver and card-carrying Oglala Lakota Sioux Indian who lives on the Pine Ridge Reservation, South Dakota—designated one of the poorest areas in America. His great-great-great-great-grandfather was Chief Red Cloud, the storied Oglala Lakota leader who oversaw successful campaigns against the US Army in 1866 and signed the 1868 Treaty of Fort Laramie, delineating the Indian Country through which DAPL now runs. Red Cloud died at Pine Ridge in 1909. The same Pine Ridge where over 250 Lakota were massacred and buried in a mass grave in 1890 at Wounded Knee; the same Wounded Knee where, in 1973, American Indian Movement (AIM) activists and supporters from every Indian nation occupied the town. Unlike the Standing Rock standoff, the Wounded Knee occupation was armed. But like the water protectors four decades later, the AIM resistance at Wounded Knee faced militarized, multi-agency law enforcement repression, followed by protracted court battles aimed at defanging and punishing the movement.

And it is with this historic struggle in mind that Freeman chose to join the camp, originally "supporting the DAPL resistance not in [her] capacity as an attorney." She told me that after seeing water protectors "brutalized by police," and recognizing the expansive need for legal support, she applied in November to work as the criminal case coordinator for the Water Protector Legal Collective (WPLC)—a group that originated in the camp to provide on-the-ground jail and legal support for arrestees and one of two interconnected, donation-funded groups that would oversee the daunting task of coordinating defense and logistics for hundreds of disparate defendants. The other, the Freshet Collective, would work largely on arrestee support, including paying nearly half a million dollars in cash bail, coordinating criminal defense, travel, accommodation, and logistics for the out-of-state lawyers and hundreds of defendants who live nowhere near the site of their court dates. Freeman moved to North Dakota for months at a time, leaving behind her family and her regular legal practice in Denver.

"For a lot of the lawyers and the defendants here, there's a spirituality and a politics involved in this fight that can't be untangled, and it would be hard to keep working without it. So much out here is hard," Freeman said. "The attorneys and legal workers who come here, we wake up every morning and put our bodies and spirits upon the gears, upon the wheels, upon the levers, upon all the apparatus of this colonial behemoth—the state violence and repression that is occurring yet again in order to deny indigenous people sovereignty over their own lands in the name of resource extraction."

The six federal defendants were charged with use of fire to commit an offense and civil disorder, stemming from events on October 27, 2017—a major date in the pipeline standoff on which 141 people were arrested. On that day, police deployed armored vehicles, lashes of pepper spray, and LRAD sound cannons to clear water protectors from one of the campsites, while barricades were set alight and DAPL equipment was damaged. The civil disorder charge is a rarely used federal statute with a fiercely political history: it was passed in the late 1960s at the height of the Black Liberation and anti-war movements; AIM members from the Wounded Knee occupation faced the very same charge.

It was not until January 23, three days after Trump's inauguration, that the Justice Department moved to file federal charges. This, Freeman said, was "no accident." Each defendant faced up to fifteen years in prison if convicted.

Meanwhile the state cases were already trickling through Morton County, with hundreds still unresolved. "The size and scope of the thing, it's overwhelming," said Freeman.

~

It's hard to imagine a starker optic disconnect than that between the dramatic spectacle of the protest camps, on the one hand, and the boxy, small-town blocks and parking lot grids that make up the nearby cities, on the other. The pipeline fight provided a visual language of indigenous resistance and frontline militarized battle: the bright flags of every tribal nation flying, the temporary tent and tipi towns, hundreds of bold banners, water protectors in traditional dress mounted on horses, law enforcement officers and National Guardsmen in riot gear. Tear gas. Water cannons. Fire.

Just over 70,000 people live in Bismarck, where the federal court is small enough to share a building with the post office—the granite stone entrance of which became a regular backdrop for protests. In bars decked in mock saloon style and American flags, "Backing the Blue: Friends of Law Enforcement" signs are posted in the windows. Neighboring Mandan has a mere 21,769 residents—slightly greater than the population of the protest camps at their largest. Mandan, named after the indigenous tribe that historically lived on that land, has a 90 percent white population and boasts the slogan "*Where the West Begins*." If you squint, it would almost appear quaint; a late nineteenth-century railroad town with morning-trimmed storefronts and saloons. But to look at it clearly is to see cheap, beige concrete facades and dilapidated motels, sports bars and chain restaurants. It was here that the lawyers and legal support workers would live and work out of a hotel turned flophouse, with a makeshift office on the ground floor. Inside the main building entrance sits an old-timey buggy car—no doubt once an ornament from the hotel days. A Christmas wreath still hung on the wall in mid spring.

The curtains were drawn over the office windows and there were no signs on the door. The legal team worked in one large room with mismatched felt sofas and plastic chairs, a shit-brown carpet, a defunct popcorn machine, and a poster of AIM activist and political prisoner Leonard Peltier pinned to the wall. According to Freeman and her colleagues, the first two buildings in which they tried to rent turned them down after hearing that they were in town to defend water protectors. "It's hostile environment here, for sure," Freeman said.

Rattler, speaking to me in April 2017, told me that in the previous weeks, on two occasions, two different unmarked cars had pulled up beside him on the street; a passenger had brandished a Glock pistol before the vehicles sped away. He said that numerous local residents had driven by and yelled, "Go home!" while he smoked on the porch. "It's funny, because I want to get out of here, too," he said. "But part of me wants to yell back, 'Go home? We were here first!'" He was staying at the home of a member of the local Unitarian Church—a small detached house near the center of Bismarck in a row of small detached houses, built in organized, anonymous, suburban-looking blocks.

I came to North Dakota three months after the February 2017 eviction. Signs had all but disappeared of the once-sprawling camps that had stood forty miles south of Bismarck. You had to look hard to find relics left on the wind-beaten, sand-brown grass—a lone cinder block bearing "#NoDAPL" in black spray paint, or razor wire piled up in a mound by the 1806 Highway, gleaming in the sun. Riot police had used the wire to surround and block off a sacred burial site named Turtle Island after water protectors crossed near-freezing water to pray there in November 2016.

I had traveled to the site with Freeman and some of her coworkers. An ebullient paralegal named Jess, wearing gold eye shadow and a floral skirt, pointed out where each of the various camp areas had stood. She hadn't returned to the site since the February eviction. Nor had Dandelion Cloverdale, a sex worker and educator from Montana who was working for the Freshet Collective to coordinate travel and lodging for defendants. Cloverdale walked around solemnly, eyes streaming from the winds blowing sideways on the plains. "It's sad coming back here, it looks so different," they said, adding, "It's hard"—a phrase I heard like a refrain during that trip.

Cloverdale had been the camp manager for the small Two Spirit Nation camp at Standing Rock, which brought together the intersection of the indigenous and LGBTQ struggle and many Two Spirit youth. "Before the occupation there were two teen suicides a month on this reservation" said Cloverdale. "During the occupation, there were none. There was promise and hope; young people believed in themselves." Native teens and young adults are 1.5 times as likely to kill themselves as the average US resident. The Standing Rock movement's guiding words, *Mni wiconi* (water is life), meant more than clean water advocacy. Water protectors and land defenders see themselves in a struggle to affirm and sustain *life*, which is as much spiritual as it is material and environmental.

Not all the lawyers and organizers were in North Dakota full-time, as Freeman was; some came for a few weeks at a time for hearings and meetings—a semi-rotating cast of legal activists who would join the close quarters of the Mandan office and apartments. Most nights they would cook and eat vegan food together, crammed into Freeman's temporary living room on two sofas and the floor. Files and paperwork took up every table surface, with extension cords and wires from four or five laptops at a time snaking around the sparse furniture. Outside of their temporary lodgings, the Freshet and WPLC workers stood out in white Trump country; their ranks included Native Americans, gender nonconforming and queer individuals, trendy New Yorkers and what your grandparents might call hippies. "I was picking someone up from Bismarck airport," Cloverdale told me, "and a group of white folks told me 'you need to go home.' They don't like out-of-towners around here; they give dirty looks to out-of-state [license] plates."

Freeman concurred. "I've never had to work as a defense attorney and endure this kind of hostile environment," she said. A longtime activist lawyer, she noted that "unlike movements we've seen recently, there's not a robust well of attorneys here. And the court system could have never anticipated this."

The state Supreme Court deemed the situation an "emergency affecting the legal system of North Dakota." Seventy defense lawyers from all over the state were appointed to cases; "typically they live and work about four hours away," Freeman said. But only about ten local defense counsel were working directly with the WPLC. With only so many barred criminal defense attorneys in North Dakota, a number of whom expressed negative bias against water protectors, the state had to change its rules to let out-of-state lawyers practice in the Standing Rock cases in what's known as a "pro hac vice" capacity. Pro hac vice lawyers must work with a barred North Dakota counsel; thus, the local lawyers working with the WPLC served as local counsel for around forty to forty-five out-of-state lawyers.

North Dakota as a whole has an entrenched conservative bent, with Republicans in firm control of the state House and executive. Local landowners and residents in the surrounding rural areas described the camps as a source of disruption, crime and vandalism.

"These were situations and circumstances we'd never seen before. It was emotionally, physically and economically taxing to the community," said Julie Ellingson, the executive vice president of the North Dakota Stockmen's Association, a trade organization that represents livestock producers. "This is a quiet, agricultural area; the largest cattle producing county in the state," said Ellingson, who has lived in the area all her life. She told me that during the time of the camps, livestock producers couldn't move their cattle from field to field, facing protest-related roadblocks and an alleged uptick in stolen, injured and killed animals.

On top of a uniquely brutal winter, these were unwelcome interruptions that provoked ire against protesters, but not the pipeline that drew them to North Dakota. Ellingson was one among a number of local residents who told me that they believed the pipeline construction abided by relevant laws, regulations and necessary agreements—a view challenged by the (equally local) Standing Rock Sioux and their federal court victory over the lack of adequate environmental studies and adherence to treaty protections. Ellingson said that locals felt like "collateral damage" in the Standing Rock standoff—an opinion echoed by Jerry Hintz, who along with his wife owns a popular local tea shop and café in Bismarck.

I met Hintz, a friendly, athletic forty-six-year-old with a shaved head and bright blue eyes, in his well-lit shop just a short walk from the federal court–cum–post office. The gray day poured in through the store's glass front, deadening any touches of coziness in the strip mall space, which shares a bland Bismarck block with a Burger King. "Nobody in the media came to talk to the locals. They didn't hear about how our businesses were affected, or about how police officers and their families were threatened," said Hintz, who had joined hundreds of North Dakotans in a "Backing to Blue" rally last November; he told me of "fierce loyalty" in the area to law enforcement and the military, speaking of "agitators," "trolls" and "criminals" from the camps; "We wanted to be left alone," he said.

Local fear and antipathy was further stoked through the concerted efforts of law enforcement officers, county authorities and mercenary security contractors (hired by DAPL owner Energy Transfer Partners) who spent months painting the water protectors as criminals and security threats. The *Intercept*'s May 2017 leaks of documents from international security firm TigerSwan confirm that its contractors, working with law enforcement agencies, carried out explicit propaganda campaigns through local news and social media to demonize the protesters.

It worked. A survey conducted by consulting firm The National Jury Project in the relevant counties—Morton and Burleigh—found that 77 percent of the jury-eligible population in the former, which covers Mandan, and 85 percent in the latter, which covers Bismarck, had already decided the water protectors were guilty. "A substantial number of the surveyed population have connections to law enforcement, the oil industry, landowners and others who have been affected by the protests," the survey results stated, noting, "Many respondents made statements indicating that they perceive protesters as a threat to community safety and described the water protectors as 'eco terrorists,' 'criminals,' and 'idiots' who 'hopefully all freeze to death.'" One hundred percent of respondents admitted prior knowledge of the issues involved in the cases. Motions were filed by attorneys in both state and federal court for a change of venue, to move the cases out of rural areas directly affected by the camps; they were denied.

For Freeman, the jury survey was a reflection of the sort of hostility she and her clients and colleagues have felt in the area, and the urgency that they be permitted to leave. "It's also why we are trying to have Rattler's bail conditions relaxed as soon as possible," she said. "This is a threatening environment."

State prosecutor Ladd Erickson, known for theatrical language in court and chain smoking outside of it, told me, "The fatigue the whole area felt—it got raw." A striking admission, from a prosecutor, about the risk of local bias. If the whole area was affected, I asked, how could impartial jurors be found for all these cases? "It's challenging," he admitted, before asserting swiftly that fair juries were nonetheless being found. He stressed that contrary to charges of racism in the area against Indians, his Native American friends ("my guys" as he called them) in the sheriff's department were also burned out by the camps. The same state's attorney filed motions in December 2017 to disallow defendants from mentioning the following in court: "historical treaties between the US Government and the Sioux Nation; tribal sovereignty; the merits and demerits of the Dakota Access Pipeline; climate change; sacred sites." Erickson argued these issues had "no relevance" to the criminal cases at hand.

If an individual defendant *did* want to raise the fact that 99 percent of the arrests took place on land accorded to the Lakota Tribe in either the 1851 or 1858 Fort Laramie treaties, the point would have had little legal traction. But if these treaties—harsh compromises in and of themselves—were truly respected, none of these trials would be happening: state and federal powers have no jurisdiction on treaty land. Indeed, if they had been historically honored, there would be no DAPL in the first place. The grim irony that many of the arrests led to trespass charges for natives on what should be their land is one that animates the history of this country.

The attorney noted that there is hardly anywhere to bring an argument from a sovereign nation's claim; international courts are not going to weigh in on the Standing Rock criminal trials. But according to the lawyers I spoke to, including Bruce Ellison—a veteran attorney who represented AIM leaders after the 1973 standoff and continues to represent Leonard Peltier as well as a number of Standing Rock defendants—many of the cases are eminently defensible on points of law and proof, regardless of a treaty defense. The challenge is to defend that which they believe to be defensible in this tough rural context, where a small legal operation has had to handle hundreds of cases.

After a group dinner in her living room one night, Freeman and I sat in her equally jumbled adjoining bedroom. "In these cases we have both law and proof on our side. But really," she said, with a quiver to her voice, "it's the righteousness of it."

~

In April 2018, WPLC published a tally of case statistics. Of the 831 arrests, 578 cases had concluded, with 337 won through dismissal or acquittal at trial; 226 water protectors have accepted some sort of pretrial agreement, but none that requires cooperation with the government in other defendants' prosecutions. Over half of these agreements were "pretrial diversions"—delayed dismissals that do not entail an admission of guilt. One hundred and forty-four trials were still to begin.

Accounting for every arrestee and finding each defendant appropriate representation constituted a mammoth task in and of itself. In the meantime, Freshet and WPLC worked with the local lawyers to build collective defense strategies around major days of mass arrests—like October 27—from which scores of protesters faced similar charges, and for which allegations of infirm arrest and police brutality were numerous.

And for the prosecutors, mass arrest days, which involved law enforcement officers from around the country and state, have proven a challenge. "The prosecution is realizing that they can't make out the elements of the charged offenses," said Moira Meltzer-Cohen, a New York–based attorney who has traveled back and forth to North Dakota to represent nine defendants with cases in state court in Mandan. "Some of their cases have been dismissed by judges, and also because, having brought in law enforcement from all over the country, those extra-jurisdictional cops made arrests, failed to complete any meaningful paperwork, went home, and are not keen to return to testify about something that happened in a chaotic environment months ago," she said, noting that without evidence showing individualized probable cause and without witnesses, the prosecution has dismissed some charges, which should never have been brought. Meltzer-Cohen, whom I've known for many years through her work on activist cases in New York, called the legal situation "a mess."

Local paper, the *Bismarck Tribune*, which skewed dramatically against protesters and in favor of law enforcement in its editorial pages, took acquittals at trial as an occasion to opine that "the system works for everyone." Meltzer-Cohen scoffed at the editorial. "They had to acquit," she said. "There was absolutely no basis for the charges."

The lawyer did not see the wave of dismissals as an outright victory, but evidence of vast police misconduct and original prosecutorial overreach. "The way the cops use arrest as a form of crowd control dovetails so neatly with the way prosecutors drain us, even without getting any results. It's such a stupid war of attrition, with such Pyrrhic victories on both ends," she said.

During the camp protests, the pipeline was dubbed "the black snake." But for the Lakota, the black snake is not just one pipeline. It harkens back to a prophecy in which a great black snake would come to the Lakota lands and devastate the earth. According to the prophecy, it would be the youth who would rise up to slay the black snake—a detail not lost on the Standing Rock Sioux youth who were the first to set up camp against the pipeline in April 2016.

"The black snake is greed and violence and oppression; we have to come together to fight more than just one pipeline to defeat the black snake," said Rattler as we sat in the warm, wood-accented living room. Depending on one's spiritual orientation, there could be either irony or destiny in the fact of Rattler's position as a high-profile defendant in the Standing Rock trials. He earned his name during his Marine Corps service in the early 1990s. One night, he was sleeping outside at boot camp in Pendleton, California—diamondback rattlesnake territory—when he felt a weight along the side of his body. He carefully felt along the mass. A six-foot-long poisonous diamondback had wedged itself, head down, along the side of his sleeping bag. In one move, Rattler grabbed his service knife, grabbed the snake, and cut off its head. His lieutenant, emerging from a tent, looked on. Rattler retells the story with gusto, a grin and dramatic hand gestures. "I was known for pissing off dangerous snakes," he said. The name Rattler stuck, now an appropriate nom de guerre for a man who came to North Dakota to fight the black snake, and whose liberty has been threatened because of it.

Back in South Dakota, Rattler worked as a truck driver and a handyman, preferring to barter his trades and skills for items he needed to live, rather than money. Ceremony was already part of his life, as an entrusted Lakota pipe carrier— an honored role in ceremonial practice and tradition. He had first come to Standing Rock to deliver donated supplies from Pine Ridge in Betty Boop (his truck, for which he uses biofuel whenever possible). He made three return trips, until one event in September 2016 prompted him to stay for good.

In early September, protesters claimed that private DAPL security guards released attack dogs and sprayed mace on protesters. A spokesperson for Energy Transfer Partners told press at the time that protesters had "attacked" its workers first, but footage of clashes between law enforcement and water protectors catalyzed national attention. "After the dog attacks I knew I had to stay; it's in my nature to want to protect people," Rattler said. Freeman nodded as she listened to him, a hand on his shoulder. In that sense, they both had stayed in North Dakota for the very same reason—as protectors.

During his months stuck in Bismarck, the water protector waited and prayed. Most days, he stayed inside, reading, writing and sketching. Rattler reread letters of support and solidarity he received from supporters around the country while he was in jail. "I even got some postcards from a woman in France," he said, leaping up to pull from a cabinet a pile of assorted, well-handled cards and papers. He has also been working on a children's book, he told me—a story about a young indigenous boy and his adventures in precolonial times.

He wants to give children "an image of what we looked like, before Hollywood made us look like savages."

"I'm not smart about a lot of things. I'm more of an action guy. But I have 100 percent trust in them," he said turning to Freeman and wrapping her in a vast hug. "My life is in their hands," he said. When we returned to her apartment above the office that night, Freeman briefly burst into tears, wiped her eyes, and got back to work.

Addendum: *As his trial neared in January 2018, Rattler made the difficult decision to take a non-cooperating plea agreement, rather than risk a minimum of fifteen years in prison were he to be found guilty at trial. In late September 2018, Rattler was sentenced to a 36-month federal prison sentence, which began in November. "I am praying that they have the strength to keep up the fight and to get more people out there," said the water protector in a press release following his sentencing. "Standing Rock was a training ground. It was started by children, by the youth. Those are the generations that we're thinking about. What are we going to leave them— birds, animals, rivers? What kind of legacy do you want to leave your children? For rich people, it's a big bank account. For me it's Mni Wiconi—water is life."*

Know Your Rights

When I wrote about the J20 arrests and charges for *Esquire* in April 2017, for a mainstream readership, I appealed to a specific type of logic—a juridical one. I stressed the infirmity of the mass arrest in the law's own terms, noting that the police failed in their duty to establish individualized probable cause (as if I would have been satisfied with the DC cops had they only been more precise in their targeting of window breakers). To communicate the injustice of the thing, and the danger its precedent posed, I talked about rights.

The arrests, I pointed out, citing civil rights organizations and constitutional lawyers, deployed collective punishment and abrogated First Amendment protections. Strategically, an appeal to free speech and assembly rights is appropriate and necessary in these cases. But as reactionary anti-protest repression heightens across the country, we do well to understand the risks and limits of a response framed by this rights discourse, which would honor only the rights of individuals who assemble in a manner deemed "peaceful" by the state.

While in cases where First Amendment activity is threatened, we may want to seek a rights defense in court, but our defense of dissent *outside* the courts should not be limited by what the state deems defensible by the metrics of protected rights. A rights discourse, for example, would not defend the deliverer of that glorious punch to Richard Spencer—it would, in fact, defend Spencer.

An overreliance on the language of First Amendment rights treats the state—the Trumpian, corporate, white supremacist state—as an interlocutor, instead of as an enemy. When we call upon the government to recognize our right to peaceful assembly, we appeal to the democratic conscience of the state. "A conscience," as British cultural critic John Berger noted in a 1968 essay in the journal *International Socialism*, "which is very unlikely to exist."

Berger highlighted a conflict inherent to the sort of public demonstrations that First Amendment rights aim to defend: "If the State authority is open to democratic influence, the demonstration will hardly be necessary; if it is not, it is unlikely to be influenced by an empty show of force containing no real threat." It's safe to say we live in a moment when it is clear and correct to distrust the state's openness to democratic influence.

Berger did not reject the significance of legal protests— which manage to show, in their peaceful numbers, the potential for revolutionary action (if very rarely)—but he saw their limitations insofar as they are empty shows of force unlikely to influence the state. A rights discourse, which is only useful to defend this sort of protest, will thus echo its main limitation: defense of that which is no real threat to the powers that be.

The J20 cases don't stand alone. In April 2017, two UN Human Rights Commission investigators issued a statement in response to the wave of bills introduced in over nineteen states following Trump's election, which can generously be deemed "anti-protest." The experts noted an "alarming and undemocratic" trend. In Indiana, for example, Republicans proposed legislation to allow police to use "any means necessary" to remove protesters from a roadway; in Virginia, lawmakers introduced a bill that would make "unlawful assembly" after the police have ordered a crowd to disperse punishable with a year's jail time; in North Dakota, Republicans proposed legislation to legalize running over protesters if they are blocking roadways. (Happily, all three bills failed.)

The investigators were particularly alarmed by an apparent failure in legal understanding running through the language of many of the proposed bills. Again and again, US lawmakers referred to the threat of "violent protest." The UN experts demurred. "There can be no such thing in law as a violent protest," the investigators wrote. "There are violent protesters who should be dealt with individually and appropriately by law enforcement. One person's decision to resort to violence does not strip other protesters of their right to freedom of peaceful assembly. This right is not a collective right; it is held by each of us individually."

In the unlikely event that any legislators listened or cared, a possible corrective course was made clear to appease these human rights concerns, prima facie, while maintaining a conspiratorial agenda to stifle dissent: edit the bill by finding and replacing "violent protest" with "violent protester(s)." As the DC prosecutors' deployment of felony riot charges against the J20 defendants makes clear, while "violent protest" may be absent from the letter of the law, the idea is operative in police tactics and court proceedings. A riot charge inherently carries the risk of collective punishment, and the "violent protest" is de facto posited as the grounds to name "violent protesters" as members.

Defendants and lawyers in cases like those from J20 have every reason to call upon the logic of the UN statement to highlight the unconstitutionality of their mass arrest. But as a broader response to the crackdowns against dissent, the UN line is not only a blunt weapon, but one with unintended consequences. In response to heightened dissent, the state further criminalizes protest; liberals then call upon a discourse of individual rights, which is useful only to defend the very mode of protest *least* suited to challenging the sort of repressive government keen to criminalize protest: this is the conflict highlighted by Berger.

Under a rights framework, the state can have its punitive way with any protester if that protester has violated some mythical social contract with "bad" or "violent" behavior.

This is dangerous in the current reality, forged by lawmakers who seek to criminalize all manner of protest activity.

When we're forced to play the state's game—that is, to bring a case to court—there's no avoiding state logic. A court doesn't care that we don't see property damage as violence. A *strategy* committed to convincing the state of the rights of "good protesters" might win some crucial battles in state houses and courts. But an *ideology* committed to the unique protection of "good protesters" (to be contrasted with "bad protesters") presumes a status quo in which we do not need to fight.

The collapse of strategy (using a rights discourse in court) into ideology (believing that defending our rights delivers real justice) recalls author-activist Arundhati Roy's concern that we've swapped a grand pursuit of justice for the far smaller demand of human rights. "Too often," Roy writes in her 2016 collection *Things that Can and Cannot Be Said*, these rights "become the goal itself ... Human rights takes history out of justice." The entire J20 black bloc was part of a struggle for justice—an explicitly anti-capitalist and anti-racist march, aesthetically unified to show symbolic and rageful opposition to everything Trump represents, on the day of his inauguration. A window breaker is no less invested in justice than a "good protester," but the individual rights discourse deployable in court is not designed to defend the former.

Reactionary state measures that abrogate individual rights produce a particular outrage from liberals, which takes the form of a certain shock. Time and again, since the beginning of the Trump presidency, I have seen political writers apoplectic over alleged rips in the Social Contract. They seem genuinely gobsmacked that the state can fall so far from its alleged foundation as a mutual agreement, forged by the will of equal pledgers. It's an almost childish disbelief. A well-meaning tantrum. A child sent to her room with no supper. *You can't do this! I have rights! We had an agreement!*

As if any state were ever birthed through peaceful agreement and democratic harmony. Is this not one of the most violent myths of the constitutional republic—that it constitutes us equally? Needless to say, it takes a certain position of privilege (or brainwashing, or both) to believe such a genealogy of state power. It's almost the liberal version of "Make America Great Again"—an appeal to a state formation and history that never was.

Friedrich Nietzsche called such liberal contractualism a "romantic illusion." He presented instead a far crueler story of state origin in which "a conqueror with the iron hand ... suddenly, and violently, and bloodily" imposes order on a previously inchoate population. For Nietzsche, the problem with the "romantic illusion" of the social contract was not only that it was a myth, but that it was a myth, like Christianity, through which we live as if it were legitimized by an unquestionable authority.

The irony is that true believers in the social contract ought, according to their own political philosophy, to withdraw their submission to a government they believe has vitiated the contract's terms. But faith in the ultimate legitimacy of the state, based in liberal contractualism, is inherently unrevolutionary: such belief relies on appeals to a government's better nature. And while there is much panic about the social contract under threat, or torn, or in tatters, there's no consistency regarding what actually constitutes its abrogation, or of what upholding the general will looks like. Are we talking Lockean or Rawlsian? A president without the popular vote? A racist prison industrial complex that disenfranchises and cages millions? The systematic roundup and removal of immigrants? Is everything legitimate except collusion with Russia?

Our rights to speak out and assemble are under attack, as the J20 arrests and numerous anti-protest bills made clear. But our defense of these rights always entails engaging on the state's terms and on the presumption of its good faith. After the Second World War, philosopher Hannah Arendt pointed out the poverty of a notion of rights as something naturally conferred on any human simply by virtue of their existence. Arendt, then writing as a stateless refugee, saw how human rights served little use to those humans stripped of or denied citizenship. The idea that human rights are protected by an international community is still dependent on the negotiation, intervention and compliance of individual states. We cannot usefully talk of rights without Arendt's famous and much-debated formulation of "the right to have rights." If the phrase sounds question begging, that's because it partly is: rights can only be conferred on those humans to whom rights are conferred. But simply put, Arendt understood that rights make no sense without recognition, and that this means recognition by state actors.

This is not to undermine, but rather to highlight, the importance of such recognition and the necessity to struggle for those who do not have it. Under Trump, this is especially daunting. But under any administration, an appeal to rights presumes the state's conscience and fealty to the social contract. The use of a rights discourse to defend against repression must be strategic and will always be limited.

When we focus too much on our rights to speak and assemble (beyond what is necessary when facing state charges and repression, as in the J20 and Standing Rock cases) our fight becomes atomized over the fact of assembly, rather than the reason for protest. Form above content. It's a fulcrum that has well suited the far right in recent years—using the Trojan horse of free speech to bring genocidal, violent content to college campuses and city squares across America.

The right of anyone to speak publicly, the neo-fascists say, is the very freedom that actual fascism would see decimated. And it is a line that has found a comfortable home with the liberal commentariat. This view finds its best iteration in that old quote so regularly misattributed to the French Enlightenment philosopher Voltaire: "I disapprove of what you say, but I will defend to the death your right to say it." (It was actually written by British Voltaire biographer Evelyn Beatrice Hall.)

It was on these grounds that the American Civil Liberties Union (ACLU) defended the Unite the Right rally's right to demonstrate at Emancipation Park in Charlottesville—work for which the ur-liberal organization received censure from anti-racist activists, especially in the wake of the August 12 terror attack, in which a self-identified white supremacist rammed his car into a crowd of counterprotesters, killing thirty-two-year-old activist Heather Heyer and injuring nineteen others. In turn, liberal commentators have jumped to the defense of the civil liberties group and the need to defend robust constitutional rights.

Much of the anger at the ACLU stems from an understandable desire that this champion of liberal and righteous causes not give time nor resources to hatemongers. Which is to misunderstand that defending neo-Nazi speech *is* profoundly liberal work, however unrighteous. In defending the civil liberties of neo-Nazi organizers, the ACLU was just doing what they say they do. The mistake is to conflate and collapse the defense of liberties with the struggle for social justice (of which the fight for equal rights is only a part).

In an August 13, 2017 article for the *Intercept*, Glenn Greenwald made a reasonable point in defense of the ACLU: that "the least effective tactic [in response to an event like Charlottesville] is to try to empower the state to suppress the expression of their views." What Greenwald left conspicuously absent, however, is that most anti-fascist "no platformers" are asking for no such thing.

The anti-fascist project, as I address in this collection's first chapter, is not one of asking for better statutes or a reconfiguration of rights. My allies who traveled to Charlottesville and then to Washington, DC, to confront Unite the Right, who shut down Milo Yiannopoulos in Berkeley, and who punched Richard Spencer are not asking Donald Trump, nor the Justice Department, nor any police department to take action against the white supremacy that undergirds their authority: Firstly, because such energy might as well be spent praying to gods that don't exist. But above all, because the history of anti-fascist, anti-racist activism is not one of presuming the good faith of state power. It is not one of asking. It is a history of direct and confrontational intervention—the sort of which is itself seldom protected by a rights framework.

Today's specious free speech debate should not lead to calls for a censorious restriction of First Amendment rights, but to an interrogation of what we can and cannot use a rights discourse to achieve. To allow white supremacists to march under the banner of "white civil rights" and "free speech" is an unconscionable authorization of racist violence. However, the answer—from a practical as well as ideological stand-point—will not come as the result of an appeal to the state to ban a far-right demonstration, rally or speech.

It's tempting to want to push for authorities to deny permits to white nationalists, like those behind the deadly Unite the Right rally in Charlottesville, out of safety concerns. Any large gathering of white supremacists is, after all, an existential threat to the lives of Black and brown people. But the bureaucracies of protest permits don't barter with *existential* safety concerns. An appeal to safety will not see most racist, fascist gatherings preemptively shut down. Nor will any appeal to governmental authority.

White supremacists *do* have a constitutional right to publicly spew hate. In a 1969 decision, the Supreme Court ruled in favor of a Ku Klux Klan member's right to call publicly for "revengeance" [*sic*] against Jews and Black people. And in 1977, the court sided with a neo-Nazi group in its attempt to march through the heavily Jewish community of Skokie, Illinois. In the Trump era, a conservative court led by Chief

Justice John Roberts is not about to overturn decades of (fascist-friendly) free speech absolutism. The government has upheld the speech rights of white nationalists with ardor. And yet for others, freedom of speech and association is increasingly under threat.

We know better than to call upon the government or the courts to ban white supremacist events, especially under this white supremacist administration. Anti-fascist activists have no interest in bolstering the state's censorial oversight, and even less faith that any such censorship would ever be applied to white supremacists.

Beyond Free Speech

In November 2019, Professor Jonathan Zimmerman spoke at the University of California, Davis, putatively to address the issue of free speech and censorship on university campuses. Zimmerman, who has previously written with feverish concern for the well-being of young Trump voters at American colleges, framed the problem along an increasingly common fulcrum in this debate: he suggested that a category mistake was being made when students and others demand that offensive speech be removed from campus discourse and certain speakers be "de-platformed," or "no-platformed." By Zimmerman's lights, this is censorship driven by the "psychologizing of politics." That is, your feelings are hurt (you social justice snowflake), and you conflate your psychic pain with a valid political stance around which to organize the permissibility or impermissibility of speech in your environment. We see a similar rhetoric play out when activists who amass to shut down far-right speakers are painted as foolishly impassioned, allowing their hot-blooded angers to overwhelm the political scene; the reasoned actor, we are told, lets even the most reprehensible figure air their putrid ideologies in our midst, confident in the argumentative and persuasive strength of anti-racist, anti-nationalist rebuttals. "Politics and psychology don't play well together," said Zimmerman; the reasoned exchange of ideas, to be judged on their relative merits, is pitched against the oversensitive, unwieldy, apolitical and unphilosophic mob.

In such a schema, you would find me on the side of the mob: I stand with those students and organizers who have, around the world, made a point of shutting down racist far-right speakers and writers who have attempted to gain purchase on campuses and in cultural institutions.

For all its confidence in reasonability, Zimmerman's problematic of free and unfree speech is deeply flawed. A more stringently analytic and interrogative approach to speech, and what makes it free or not—indeed how it functions as speech at all—should lead one to see reason on the side of the "deplatformers." On the side of the free speech absolutists, meanwhile, lies a quite fanciful and underthought understanding of no less than how language and meaning work. The category mistake is with those like Zimmerman, who point to the issue of "psychologizing politics" but in fact mislocate the problem entirely. The more rigorous philosophy is on the side of the mob.

The most valid positions for expelling white supremacist speech—which, to be sure, constitutes white supremacist organizing—have been well made, again and again, most particularly by communities of color, trans activists, and undocumented people who have attested to the immediate harm done to them when such voices' presence is legitimized via a public platform. These communities should no longer need to debate the mattering of their lives. I agree with this, marrow deep. But since their positions have been dismissed as over emotional and anti-intellectual, I make this argument here to meet free speech absolutists on their own proclaimed terms. Those who claim "reason" is on their side are in fact the purveyors of a near-religious and under-interrogated view of these language games.

There are a few things I want to do here. First, I want to interrogate the assumptions implicit in the common concept of permissible and "free" speech deployed by defenders of the ability for far-right speakers to speak in public or publish in mainstream platforms. Then I want to suggest an alternative, and I believe better, framework for thinking about the work done by certain types of speech—for this I'll rely upon (and support) philosopher Ludwig Wittgenstein's meaning-as-use approach, along with some simple speech act theory, and I'll appeal to just a dash of proof from recent history. I hope to establish that a more robust discussion of speech acts and linguistic scenes supports arguments to shut down racist far-right speech in public; without this, a more just society can be neither performed nor practiced.

Let me lay out some parameters; a necessary preamble, if you will. Or, if I'm honest, a preemptive response to a tired counterargument. I'm not interested here in arguing for any sort of changes to, or curtailment of, the First Amendment. My argument pertains to how communities should better organize their thoughts and actions around the sorts of speech and assembly they enable and tolerate. How we might recognize our responsibilities for creating certain political realities in the spaces in which we live, learn and work. The museum, the university administration, the newspaper, the social media company: these institutions can and do uphold stricter standards than the state—in some ways—when it comes to permitting or banning certain types of speech.

Furthermore, as I'll go on to address: we're dealing with something slippery, dynamic and contextual: that is, speech. Sure, an institution could expand its set of banned symbols and phrases (Pepe the Frog as well as the Swastika). But the administration, or the state, by changing the rules of permitted speech, would fail to arrest the dynamic of white supremacist speech acts and their adaptability. Language games do have rules—if completely contravened, we fail to make meaningful speech together, producing mere noises—but the "rules" are exceedingly malleable. These games are not a chaotic free-for-all, but they're not chess either. If there's consensus around a new convention of usage among a linguistic community, we can keep talking; if not, communication fails. What gets to count as "correct play" in language is malleable but nonetheless dependent on a critical (enough) number of participants "playing along." As Wittgenstein knew, "the meaning of a word is its use in the language."

I want to begin by recalling the words of US Supreme Court Justice Oliver Wendell Holmes Jr. in his famed 1919 dissent in the case of *Abrams v. United States*—a text that has, perhaps more than any other, undergirded legal thinking around freedom of speech in America and beyond for the last century. "The best test of truth," wrote Holmes, "is the power of the thought to get itself accepted in the competition of the market." Holmes was a pragmatist and a careful judicial thinker. But today we see his dissent reduced into an under-thought premise for free speech absolutism. Given the chance to compete with each other in this "marketplace of ideas," the best ideas, indeed the truth, will win through; as such, it must be this marketplace, rather than some censorious authority or "mob," that determines which ideas are given a platform. The least and most we can and should do, according to such a framework, is to keep the marketplace open.

The overused market analogy—or market ideology—informs modern First Amendment doctrine, and constitutes the under-examined framework of today's free speech debate. It is this framework, not the legal doctrine itself, that I'm interested in taking to task. It is a weak understanding of how speech, truth and meaning works. Indeed, for a debate around speech, in which the university campus is the terrain of contest, it's pretty astounding how little theoretical attention has been given to the functioning of speech. It's as though decades—*centuries*—of philosophical work were somehow irrelevant in the face of only partially applicable, barely interrogated, liberal judicial ideology.

In July 2020, *Harper's Magazine* published a "Letter on Justice and Open Debate" signed by over 150 writers, academics and public figures—including anti-trans zealot J.K. Rowling, scholar-activist Noam Chomsky, novelist Margaret

Atwood and a host of exceedingly bad conservative and liberal thinkers like Steven Pinker and Malcolm Gladwell, alongside other paranoiac centrists fearing so-called cancel culture. Published during a potent moment of Black liberation struggle, when, finally, the institutional racism and whiteness of so many established media institutions was under the spotlight, the letter argued that speech was under threat. This threat came from authoritarian impulses of Donald Trump, the letter noted, but its real focus was the "censoriousness" of the anti-racists and anti-fascists, who have dared demand that racism and anti-trans hate no longer be considered valid terrains of public debate. "It is now all too common to hear calls for swift and severe retribution in response to perceived transgressions of speech and thought," stated the letter—a most vicious deployment of the word "perceived." The letter echoes Holmes's dissent almost verbatim, as if his proposition were unquestionable: "The way to defeat bad ideas is by exposure, argument, and persuasion, not by trying to silence or wish them away."

A number of presumptions underlie this standardized approach to free speech. First, it presumes that this thing called the "market" is a fair judge of goodness and truth; that it is a fair organizer of justice. Such free market fundamentalism is roundly decried, and is indeed laughable when applied to an economic context (and it is an economic analogy); in the aftermath of (just the latest) ferocious financial crisis, faith in the market as a fair arbiter is nothing but the near-religious preserve of the mega-rich—those who have benefited from what a deeply unfair terrain it is. Yet we continue to treat the market analogy as unproblematic when applied to speech and ideas; we have no grounds to do so and ample empirical bases to see the operations of "the marketplace of ideas" as equally rigged to favor existing power structures. Any claim otherwise finds itself in the terrain of what Jamaican philosopher Charles W. Mills calls "white ignorance": that well-fostered individualist epistemology, where stories of truth telling conveniently forget the facts of history. At one point, for example, in German-colonized South West Africa, white settlers demanded "that in court only the testimony of seven African witnesses could outweigh evidence presented by a single white person." Or to raise more recent examples, we might point to the numerous Palestinian scholars, and any critics of Israeli state violence, who have been fired or denied the ability to speak through claims equating anti-Zionism, or indeed mild condemnation of Israel's extreme aggressions, with anti-Semitism. It has always been the case that the ideas "marketplace" has reflected existing systems of power. So tell me again about "best of truth" winning through by virtue of this market's determinations? Such pretenses, that there exists a neutral terrain on which ideas merely "compete" and that the "best" will win through, require a most fanatical lack of empiricism.

Second, the "free exchange of ideas" framework posits "truth" as something that is simply there, lying around to be found, to win the day. The framework thus ignores the dead, real, material conditions—the brutal hierarchies—that organize what gets to be truth. A more "critical" approach to truth telling by no means denies the existence of verifiable facts but insists that attention is given to the "activity" of speech: who gets to do it, how, where and to whom. This isn't relativism with regard to truth; it's materialism, with a long-established history in the philosophy of science. A reckoning is in order with the limitations of facts in the face of disinterested power—the limitations of the language game of factual reporting in the face of the language game of white supremacist propagandizing.

Third, and more to the point here, the absolutist model locates speech—the unit that is to be deemed permissible or not—in a specific way. There are "thoughts" that get themselves "accepted" into the marketplace of ideas or not. These "thoughts" are the bearers of truth, falsity, merit or violence. Speech (whether verbal, written, or otherwise), then, is to be understood as that which conveys thoughts. There is the world, ideas about the world—which can be offensive or not, and true or not—and the speech that delivers those ideas. What we have here is a deeply rudimentary "conceptual" model of meaning, in which words simply attach to or represent the world (or fail to do so). Under such a static model, speech itself is merely a tool—equally available to all—with which we exchange ideas about the world. And if this is how meaning works, then sure, an absolutist free speech argument makes sense: the world and its truth is as it is, while bad ideas about it—poor or incorrect representations of it in speech—will be shown to be false when held up against better representations of the truth of the world. Fear not; abhorrent ideas and theories, like race realism, will be felled by the sheer fact of being false, perverse representations of humanity and difference.

Funny, though, that race realism hasn't been felled, even though it has been so fully discredited. Maybe we just haven't delivered our "better," more just representations of the world with sufficient clarity. Maybe we simply need to debate harder. Or, just maybe, the model of communication we're relying on here is in itself false: maybe we're actually not talking about exchanging ideas about the world. Because, I submit, when far-right figures and groups gather and speak in the public sphere, on- and offline, they're not simply positing ideas about how they believe the world is and should be, offering their thoughts up to the marketplace of ideas to be earnestly considered and judged. Or, more precisely, they *are* describing the world as they believe it to be, but that is nevertheless the least relevant aspect of the speech acts at play in such a circumstance. It is high time we stop perpetuating the myth that this is a debate about, well, when it's appropriate to *debate*.

After all, a speech act is not simply the spoken representation of a thought about the world, but the performance of an action. Like many speech acts, those performed by white supremacists in public are what the philosopher of language J.L. Austin called perlocutionary acts: that is, they are not so much organized around expressing the interiority of the speaker, or describing something, as much as they are organized around the listener—their force is their perlocutionary effect. Here's a perlocutionary speech act: "I'm hungry!" I'm not telling you I'm hungry because I want you to simply know it. I'm not in a doctor's office after stomach complications, speaking in order to describe an internal experience. I'm telling you I'm hungry for the perlocutionary effect of you thinking you should get me food. When a white nationalist says (falsely) that a "flood" of undocumented immigrants are spreading crime and taking resources, they are indeed offering a false description of the world, the falseness of which can and has, time and again, been pointed out. But the speech act is more significant in its perlocutionary force and effect: the utterance doesn't primarily function as a description, to be tested for truth of falsity; the listener (if a white European) is being told to feel threatened, and if non-white, non-European, is, in turn, being threatened by being named as a threat external to the direct audience. What's going on here, when these speech acts are enacted, is not (again borrowing from Wittgenstein) best read through "the language game of reporting." The speech acts of expressing and spreading fascistic, white supremacist desires are not parts of the language game we might call the "open exchange of ideas."

The most obvious response is: Why not simply respond with better speech acts? "Speak truth to perlocutionary effect," if you will. I want to specifically address why racist, homophobic, transphobic, anti-immigrant speech acts—qua speech acts—are not best combated with *debate*.

On the level of speech acts, I borrow from feminist philosopher Mary Kate McGowan. McGowan has offered up some banal and flawed criticisms of sex work and pornography, but I find her work useful here. She notes that to try to remove racism, misogyny, transphobia and other oppressive speech from a linguistic scene is like "unringing a bell"—that is, it's much easier to introduce sexist and racist presuppositions into a conversation than it is to exorcise them. They are what is known as "exercitive speech acts"—they determine what sort of actions or behaviors are permissible in a given domain. The police make a lot of exercitive speech acts; so do judges, umpires and referees. But there are all kinds of other quotidian examples: like when a group of acquaintances are having dinner, and one attendee starts talking about sex, so everyone feels permitted to talk about sex. There's no going back to the point before the topic was raised. But the stakes of the introduction of oppressive speech into a space are, meanwhile, the pernicious matter at hand.

Just "raising questions" about racist pseudoscience, as well as outright white supremacist speeches, involve illocutionary acts (that is, speech acts that perform deeds when uttered, like promising, declaring or commanding) that enact what McGowan calls "oppressive permissibility facts." From the speech acts of Richard Spencer's invocation of "white pride" and Milo Yiannopolous's mockery of trans students, to the speech act of Charles Murray's suggestion that white men are intellectually superior, or that of Senator Tom Cotton urging the military be deployed against Black American protesters —these all enact, even if not explicitly, the permissibility of oppression in the environment in which they're spoken. The perlocutionary effect of Trump's racist speech, that is, the attendant huge spike in white supremacist hate crimes, should make this clear. And again, conversations are asymmetrically pliable: there's a general asymmetry between verbally making something salient (by which I mean noticeable) as part of a linguistic scene or terrain, and verbally making something un-salient. Un-ringing a bell, putting toothpaste back into the tube. Calls for the free exchange of ideas, appeals to capital-T truth, wholly fail to reckon with asymmetric pliability and the introduction of oppressive permissibility facts. That is to say, free speech absolutism again fails to understand how speech works. Those who have felt the brute force of this "introduction of oppressive permissibility facts"—that is, the vile lived reality of racism—don't need speech act theory to understand this. It's a shame so many cultural, institutional and educational gatekeepers still do.

Let's look at the language games at play in the following example. When, in response to the many, many executions, beatings and cagings of Black people by police and the criminal justice system, thousands rose up to assert "Black lives matter!" The call was for a truth that has not been, has never been, instantiated in the United States or the West more generally: Black lives have not been permitted to matter. In response, the worst reactionaries and stupidest centrists asked why we could not instead make the call "All lives matter!" It's a true statement, to be sure: all lives do matter. But under the current and violent order of things, all lives don't get to matter; by parrying the specificity of Black lives and working as a rejoinder, the utterance, albeit true, commits its own violence. The meaning of a statement is in its use, and the call is deployed not in the language game of describing the mattering of lives, but in the maintenance of brutal, racist hierarchies in which Black lives don't get to matter. "Black lives matter!," as a speech act, is not *primarily* in the service of description either; it's a demand, to be repeated until it doesn't need saying anymore.

I'm interested in these language games of resistance and how we play them. That's why I, and many others, use the word "fascist" to describe Donald Trump, his advisor Stephen Miller, the alt-right Reform UK (née Brexit Party) leader Nigel Farage and the German Alternative für Deutschland, among others. We could simply call them far-right nationalists and racists, and we do that, too. Those who claim these figures do not fit a formal definition of "fascism," however, miss the fact that, as I noted in chapter 1, fascism is a family-resemblance concept—and these characters and groups certainly share in "a network of similarities" with what was historically described as "fascist." And many of us who use the term "fascism" today do so in order to invite an anti-fascist response, a response of resolute intolerance, to the fascistic constellations we're seeing. This too is a speech act, not only a description; it's an aggressive and ethical move to draw and redraw the boundaries of what we might call "fascist" as we go.

It's worth noting that the contemporary far right, metastasizing online, often uses the pliability of meaning to its advantage. Consider, if you will, the "okay" hand symbol (index finger and thumb held in a ring): far-right trolls laughed at liberals who "fell" for the supposed hoax of believing the "okay" hand sign to be a white supremacist gesture. But since it was white supremacists who kept "okaying" in photos, it turns out the social justice snowflakes were correctly observing a new hate symbol's addition to the lexicon through the far right's collective use. In response to alleged political correctness gone too far, the vile alt-right radio host Paul Joseph Watson once tweeted, "Wearing a sombrero is not racist, you utter dolt. It's a fucking hat." Against this sort of disingenuous appeal to "factual" meaning as a cover for racism, we can say to those playing Watson's game: Look, you utter fascists, meaning is use—it's not just a fucking hat.

One might respond: "But hey, it's not like far-right speakers today would be introducing white supremacist ideology by extolling it publicly; these aren't new ideas! They undergird the history of Europe and the United States. So since the bell has been rung, and rung and rung, we can't pretend to not have ever heard it." This rebuttal, however, misses the difference between citationality—the ability to cite and discuss a given discourse without restating or reasserting its claims—and each new (oppressive) speech act. I'm not suggesting that we don't talk about and discuss white supremacist ideology; we're doing it now, and to do so requires white supremacist speech to be in some sense citationally available, in order for us to know what it has looked like, currently looks like, how it persists and changes and warps. But this does not mean that speech acts of the far right on campuses, online and in public are thus useful in exposing us to these ideas. Rather, they're overexposed: their speech acts function only to introduce oppressive permissibility facts into a given locale, a given community. And this is precisely the language game that must not be entertained. Indeed, the work of vigorous, loud, disruptive, sometimes-confrontational protest is deployed precisely to ensure that the insidious language game of enacted white supremacist permissibility facts is deemed too intolerable to play.

Love According to the State

When I opened the Priority Mail envelope, its contents made me cry: a hard plastic card, my photo overlaying a background of Lady Liberty's face. "Permanent Resident." My green card was in my hands after three years of paperwork, interviews with stern-faced immigration agents, a joyous wedding and a painful divorce. If my experience with US Citizenship and Immigration Services (USCIS) has taught me one thing, it is this: Do not underestimate the importance of marriage to the state.

Indeed, marriage is the only union that the federal government will recognize, the only status by which committed couples with a non-American partner can stay in the country together. And as the cruelty of the Trump administration's immigration policies makes clearer by the day: Do not underestimate the power the state has to rip apart the families it does not want to recognize.

I didn't have a green card marriage. I did get a marriage green card. The process to get it, as anyone who has gone through it might attest, was a dizzying, panic-inducing bureaucratic obstacle course—a strange lesson in state determinations of love and partnership.

A 2012 *New York Daily News* article on the officials who interrogate couples applying for green cards wrote, "The green-card gumshoes use old-fashioned sleuthing to ferret out marriages of convenience from cases of true love." They don't. They use paperwork and presumptions; it's the couple that does the work. "True love" as recognized by the United States

Citizenship and Immigration Services is an uncomfortable act to perform, with little relation to any proof of love we might see as generative or affirming. It involves shared bank accounts (even though most American-citizen married couples I know have separate bank accounts), rent stubs, shared insurance. It's best if you own property together. Love, according to the state, is an asset merger.

Proof of love, when it comes to immigration, is in this sense specific. But the state adds a pernicious, ephemeral clause: the idea, my lawyer told me, is to show not only that you *are* (appropriately) married, but that you *would have gotten married anyway*. It's an important hypothetical, which technically gives the government insurmountable leverage. Proving what you would have done anyway is impossible, and this is the catch. That possible world—in which borders and governments don't threaten to tear apart people who love each other —is too far from this one to speculate over. I don't know what I might do there; and what place marriage would have in such a world is another question entirely.

When amassing evidence of love for the USCIS, a couple essentially aims for a facsimile of doing what *people who get married anyway* do—which, going by government guidelines, refers to anachronistic, income-stable, middle-class American Dream aspirants. Such people barely exist among all-American couples, let alone green card hopefuls, but the simulation persists between the lines of USCIS guidelines for proof. Rom-com depictions—such as 1990's *Green Card*, starring Gérard Depardieu—could lead one to believe that the interviews deal in the important banalities of living and loving together. How does he like his tea? What TV shows do you watch? The government doesn't care about the color of your toothbrushes.

My ex-husband and I began living together soon after we met in a short-lived Brooklyn squat, one year after I'd moved from London to New York for graduate school. We never signed a lease together. We shared beds, rooms, whole apartments, for months and weeks in Manhattan, Brooklyn and (for a drab nine months) in DC. Paychecks and bank statements went to a spread of friends' houses and old addresses. We barely spent a night apart in three years, but we lacked the records to prove it. Following our lawyer's advice, we opened a joint bank account and ensured mail was delivered with both our names. Raised a denizen of the internet, I don't have a lot of hard-copy photographs. I only own one photo album, and it's tucked away in a box file on a shelf that I can't even reach. I've rarely looked at the crimson binder of amateur snapshots—my wedding album—compiled for the perusing eyes of a federal agent.

A New York–based, white couple—one male, one female, with the green card applicant from Britain—rarely run the immigration gauntlet. The Trump administration, and the Obama administration before that, make very clear which immigrants will be persecuted, which loves and marriages will not pass muster. Mine was not a story about enduring persecution. Under Trump, even undocumented immigrants applying for green cards through their longtime American spouses are now targeted for deportation, including when the marriage is recognized as legitimate. Fabiano de Oliveira, a Brazilian man, was arrested by ICE as he sat with his wife, the mother of his five-year-old son, in the United States Citizenship and Immigration Services; he was in the process of applying for his legal permanent residency. Under the malignant guidance of White House advisor Stephen Miller, US immigration policy is directed toward ethnic cleansing.

Six years ago, I received my conditional green card without many issues. Two years later, when it was time to apply for permanent resident status, I was in the midst of a divorce, following months of the sort of violent decline that marks many *real* but unsustainable intimacies. "Fake" relationships for immigration purposes are unlikely to dissolve with violent fights and a partner's hospitalization for attempted suicide (this is a story for later). Nonetheless, the legitimacy of our original union (the condition for my permanent residency, even after divorce) came under suspicion; I fought to prove it and, eventually, succeeded. My marriage, no shorter than many, was recognized.

Marriage is a proprietary and abolition-worthy institution. I thought that before, during and after my first marriage. I think it now. And yet I will marry again. I will not let a border separate me from my current partner, the man with whom I will spend my life. I'm against marriage, but, dear reader, I'm looking forward to marrying him. I wept at my brother's wedding and trembled at my first. In the words of magnificent writer and critic Andrea Long Chu: "Perhaps my consciousness needs raising. I muster a shrug. When the airline loses your luggage, you are not making a principled political statement about the tyranny of private property; you just want your goddamn luggage back."

Marriage maintains a stubborn place in the romantic imaginary, and an immovable one in the state's terrain of recognition. This underlines the importance of the US Supreme Court's 2015 ruling to legalize same-sex marriage. My first thought after the *Obergefell v. Hodges* ruling was of green cards. To deny same-sex partners access to marriage, and thus access to state recognition, is discrimination, pure and simple; *Obergefell* was a necessary victory and one we must fight to protect against an ever more right-wing Supreme Court bench. Queer revolutionaries have every reason to disdain their historic struggle's contemporary focus on assimilation to the archaic institution of marriage (and the right to serve in the military). Stonewall—the 1969 uprising that inaugurated the LGBTQ movement in the United States—was a riot. But if a central problem with marriage is the state's hegemonic control over which people and sets of relationships get recognized, and get to stay, then the problem is with such operations of power, not with individuals' pursuit of equal rights and liberties within such a system.

I'd heap confetti on any couple who had wanted to legally marry but could only do so after the 2015 Supreme Court ruling. For those who found resonance in then-Justice Anthony Kennedy's words on the "transcendent purposes of marriage": let the champagne flow, although I challenge your understanding of the meaning of "transcendental." Kennedy's panegyric to marriage as a form of existential identification with another human is of little interest to the immigration agents who decide what counts as "real" marriage and which partners get to live in this country.

In the case of state-recognized marriage, we're talking about the attainment of recognition from an institution that wields power over us. We can hate this, and work to fight against it, while nonetheless appreciating the exigencies of navigating it now. We cannot underestimate the current necessity of state recognition, and what it feels like to obtain it. It is why I can sit and write, US soil beneath me. It is bright relief, which should be denied no one—relief, of course, predicated, as ever, on fear.

Policing Desire

I want to share a couple of personal anecdotes. I don't mean them to be confessions in the sense that Foucault used the term "confessional"—as the alleged revelations of some Truth from the depths of myself or my experience. But these are sex stories (kinda), and Foucault noted that sex—what we talk about when we talk about sex—takes the privileged form of confession in our society.

So perhaps I can't, we can't, talk about sex non-confessionally; it's a discourse constructed on the idea of revelation. That's how truths about sex, or anything, are built—in the false belief that they are "found." And that's what these sex stories are about: the myth of revelatory sex, and the truths it produces.

One is about a threesome I didn't have; another is about certain porn that I don't watch. They both involve an ex-partner I dated from my early to mid twenties who believed in revolutionary sex to the point of ideology. These are cautionary tales in how easily invocations toward radical sexual practices —especially in the context of political movements—can be recuperated into patriarchal power structures, technocapital, and the creation of more bourgeois desiring machines. And through them, I want to question what it means to talk about radical sex being recuperable at all.

What, if anything, was radical in the first place?

At a time when technology presents itself as playing the libera-tory function of pluralizing sexual possibilities, it's important to question the underlying idea that abundance—of partners and perversities—equals liberation. On the other hand, I don't want to fall into a trap that denies the possibility of radical modes of sexually relating to each other, just because seemingly "radical" sexual preferences and identities are easily accessible on the App Store or on a porn tube site. These are open questions, but they give lie to claims about the *inherent* radicality of certain sexual practices—a lie too often peddled by the bombastic men-children and self-satisfied sex-posi "adventurers" spanning from the far left to the Burning Man playa.

This ex and I were together during Occupy and involved in New York's fractured anarchist scene, which briefly held itself together with school-glue solidarity for a few heady months. We were nonmonogamous but had hardly acted on it, aside from a couple of threesomes with other women, the sort of which I've had in numerous relationships with men without this ex's radical posturing.

He spoke a big game about "queering." About challenging a social order organized by heteronormative and coupled forms. He saw a political imperative in pursuing polyamorous and queer constellations. In (what seemed to be) queer porn (more on this later), and in kink, he saw revolutionary interventions. Sometimes he used "queer" to mean a political subjectivity that works to undo both hetero- and homo-normativities—queer-as-disruption, as opposed to gay-as-assimilation: "Not gay as in happy, queer as in 'fuck you.'" Sometimes he used "queer" to describe any sexual interaction between non-straight, non–conventional-bodied, or non-cisgendered folks—"queer" as in a label you can use to identify yourself on an app designed for threesomes. Both meanings exist, and they intersect—his problem was that he collapsed them together entirely. (His problem was also alcohol.)

I, too, believe that a heteronormative social order that *punishes* desires, identities, and sexual practices outside of its narrow remit must be burned to the ground. Individuals and communities have fought and died, and still do, to be able to love and fuck without persecution. The work of queer pornographers to give these desires representation and recognition is crucial.

And, of course, to join a movement to fight persecution is the very meaning of becoming a political subject. Times of political revolt have long been attended by claims about the revolutionary force of challenging traditional sexual prescriptions. And little wonder: sex is a discourse that plays a major role in shaping what kinds of selves get to exist and how they get to exist together. This is the stuff of politics.

The problem with my ex's position was modal. He viewed certain sex—certainly not all sex—as a *necessary* rite of passage, without which appropriate radicalization was impossible. His belief touched on the religious—a faith that certain sex acts between certain bodies carried a radically transformative quality, a priori. For a man who claimed to be a Foucault scholar, it was a baffling assertion of normative moral facts. But we met when I was very young. He was twelve years my senior, and it took me some time to weed out the hypocrisy and dogmatism from what, if anything, was righteous, or even sexy.

People say "the personal is political" a lot, and almost always in a reductive way. It doesn't *just* mean that our individual "personal" issues—like our sexuality, our families, our fucking —are political negotiations. Is it even useful to call these "personal" issues? Aren't impersonal issues also political? And if that's the case, then everything is political, so why use the word to delineate anything at all?

Perhaps like this: the personal is political because personhood is political. Who gets to be a person, and how? How are persons formed, categorized, and organized in and through relations with each other? The personal is not political because personal choices are necessarily political choices, but because the very terrain of what gets to be a choice and what types of persons get to be choosers—what types of persons get to *be*—are shaped by political power. The sort of political power that whispers through human histories of convention formation and maintenance, of hierarchy and adherence to it, of regimes of expertise, of oppression, of struggles and paradigm shifts.

Remember how Meryl Streep's character (editor in chief of an influential fashion magazine) in *The Devil Wears Prada* chastises Anne Hathaway's character (the naive assistant) for thinking she had agency when she'd chosen to buy a blue sweater? A Foucauldian point well made: capital didn't *make* her choose and buy that color sweater, but it did overdetermine the conditions of possibility for any such purchase.

And so it is with our sexual desires: we think we *just have them*, as if there are not centuries of power operations determining our desiring tendencies—as well as the very terrain of what gets to be a choice, and who gets to be a chooser. The risk of a personal-is-political discourse that focuses on individual choice, rather than on terrains of choice making, is the development of a politics that finds its primary expression through, say, buying organic or downloading an app for nonmonogamous fucking that allows you to define yourself as "pansexual." *Who you are* is held stable, while your personal choices are deemed political. This is what I call "neoliberal identity politics"—another phrase used a lot these days, and almost always incorrectly.

So back to this ex.

After one of the many days of vigorous street protest during Occupy's heyday, a large group of anarchists were reviewing, recuperating, and relaxing in a Brooklyn loft space often used for such purposes. I had to leave reasonably early to wake up for a radio interview of some sort. My ex stayed late and ended up going home with another person (who then identified as female, but no longer does). And, as far as he explained it the following day, the assumption had been that I would join them in bed the next day.

The particulars of our nonmonogamy at that time (not all nonmonogamies are the same) required that he inform me in advance of going home with another person. Since I had been asleep, this was not possible, and his unopened texts could hardly be said to count. So that was a fuckup on his part. And it's a fuckup particular to our technological moment: instant communication has never been so easy, producing at times a misleading presumption that we have communicated—or should have been able to communicate—information to an intended party simply by sending it. The speech acts fail, and digital enmeshment is curbed by the timeless human predicament of being asleep.

This isn't just an issue when communicating polyamorous plans—it's a problem of an expectation being produced. Expectations of reception and response didn't emerge with the invention of instant messaging; centuries of waiting on tenterhooks for letters preceded this. But I think the assumption of instantaneousness produces an often-incorrect feeling that the sender has successfully communicated. In this case, he had not.

The far-greater violation, by my lights, was his assumption that I would want to have sex with this person, and his acting on that assumption; he said this was the condition under which they went home together. Moreover, that I *should* want to have sex with this person because they were, as he put it, "queer and cool."

The arguments that followed didn't focus on the problematics of his assuming my desires for me. They turned on the fulcrum of why my desires weren't somehow better. I wasn't attracted to this person, so my ex called me a body fascist. My ex might be right. My libidinal tastes fit firmly within conventional determinations of beauty. I could, and often do, look back on this story as an ur-example of a manarchist (as they are known) weaponizing the idea of radical sexual politics in order to police the desires of others to serve his own.

And that's all true. No one should be expected to fuck anyone. But this is complicated by the fact that sometimes our desires *are* worth questioning and challenging. Sometimes experimentation, while it should be conditional on consent, *does* require trying things we might not immediately *desire* in and of themselves, but as potential introductions to desiring differently. *Don't know what I want but I know how to get it.*

But by treating sex as a political project of rupturing pre-conditioned desires, might we end up reducing each other to experimental objects for our own self-development? And more to the point, such an approach treats sex *acts* as techniques of self-construction, as if the simple meeting of certain bodies serves to subvert and reorganize desires. Maybe it can. Maybe I think there are more urgent political projects than having sex with people I don't currently find attractive, but who share my political diagnoses. And what demarcates political sex from the sort of privileged play of Burning Man orgies? Post festum, does the world look that different? I knew this would get confessional.

In a skewering 2015 essay for *Mask Magazine*, the writer who goes by FuckTheory coined the term "queer privilege," as if he'd had my ex in mind. He notes that while "there is still a bigoted wide world out there, full of enforced normativity, compulsory heterosexuality, and relentless, violent policing … there are also spaces … where a generalized ideology of anti-normativity holds sway, queerness is a badge of honor, a marker of specialness, and a source of critical and moral authority: in short, a form of privilege." FuckTheory's conten-tion with what he calls queer privilege is that such attitudes, and the deep irony of their basis in a misunderstanding of Foucault, are "grounded in the idea of a link between the nor-mativity of an act and its ethical valence."

He puts it better than I ever could: "It's worth pausing to reflect on the tone that queer privilege indulges itself in, to consider the implications of a smug condescension that presumes to judge people's sexuality based on the way they relate to other people's genitals and to evaluate the revolutionary potential of an act based on its statistical prevalence. Is this what we want from queer theorizing?" The counterargument to queer privilege is not to retreat to the reactionary normativities that queerness, even privileged queerness, attempts to disrupt. No, the radical thing is not *actually* to be a straight couple and get married and make babies and reproduce oneself as the world produced you. It's not actually more radical to be monogamous just because everyone and their panamorous triad is meeting in an expensive bar in Williamsburg and reveling in their radical performance. Such a counterreaction would merely repeat the problem of inherently linking the normativity or abundance of a given act with its ethical weight.

It's a problem well put in anonymously authored text *The Screwball Asses*, published by queer theorist Guy Hocquenghem. "Will any desire, apart from obedience, ever be able to structure itself otherwise than as transgression or counter-transgression?" notes the 1973 text. "Limiting oneself to a sexual path, under the pretext that it is one's desire and that it corresponds to a political opportunity for deviance, strengthens the bi-polarization of the ideology of desire that has been forged by the bourgeoisie." The *Screwball Asses* author didn't need to live in the time of Grindr, Tinder, Bumble, or Feeld to know that "there is no escaping economics ... Roles are not broken but granted." The irony: the ex gave me that book.

Which brings me to my second anecdote—more of a string of instances.

This same ex used to watch a decent amount of porn. We'd watch together, but more often to discuss it than to get off with each other. His perversions were not mine. And yes, his tastes were more queer. And he would find his tastes represented—this is a good thing. But his means of viewing were, as with the majority of porn viewers, through a set of reductive search categories on behemoth tube sites like YouPorn, Pornhub, and RedTube, all of which are owned by one monopolizing content delivery giant, MindGeek.

It was not his *fault*, per se, that tube sites rely on a grim taxonomy of racist, sexist, transphobic, ageist, and ableist tropes: "big Black," "Asian teen," "thug," "schoolgirl," "MILF," "shemale," and so on. But it was a telling dissonance: he would praise the radical content, while using the very tube sites that have decimated the porn industry, reinforced its archaic categories, and undermined workers' rights.

Some years later, I became friendly with some of the actors and directors whose content would sometimes pop up (stolen) as a tube site click in the ex's searches. I have written about their efforts to challenge porn's problematic search tags, as well as their Homeric and often-thwarted attempts to improve working conditions. And while porn workers in the straight and queer sides of the industry challenge the means of their industry's production and its conservative business model, it is all too often that the mere abundance of transgressive content is misread as revolutionary.

Writing about porn in 2004, film theorist Linda Williams rightly noted that "as the proliferating discourses of sexuality take hold ... there can no longer be any such thing as a fixed sexuality—male, female, or otherwise." She wrote that "now there are proliferating sexualities," and that "the very multiplicity of these pleasures and perversions inevitably works against the older idea of a single norm—the economy of the one—against which all else is measured." And insofar as there is no longer one "single norm," she had a point.

But the multiplicity of represented pleasures and perversions has not ended the fact of "female, male, or otherwise" sexuality (by which I presume she meant gender). Proliferating perversions, as represented in categories of online viewing and participation, may have created a multitude of norms, but this has not meant a disruption in the hierarchical powers that control which sexual identities get represented.

And don't speak to me about radical sexual preferences if you claim to care about intersectional struggle but search "BDSM gang bang" on a tube site of stolen content, which directly hurts workers, and which runs on a taxonomy of violently reductive tags.

A survey conducted by Pornhub and *Mic* aiming to review the porn choices of millennials (of course) found that "'ebony' and 'Black' were among the top 12" of their favorite search terms. *Mic*'s hot take was that the youths were, happily, not privileging white bodies. But, as I wrote for the *Nation* at the time: there's an inherent limitation to the progressiveness of such a porn landscape if bodies are primarily sought, categorized, and thus sexualized via their race. Especially when production companies still put a premium—with pay scales and exclusivity agreements—on "interracial" scenes (almost always a white woman and a Black man), inscribing racism, through the notion of taboo, into the back end of the business.

In a dismissive and cursory 2015 essay titled "Your Sex Is Not Radical," writer and activist Yasmin Nair rejects the relevance of sexual practices in political organizing. I agree with her when she asserts, "The sad truth that many of us learn after years in sexual playing fields (literally and figuratively) is that how many people you fuck has nothing to do with the extent to which you fuck up capitalism." But her totalizing view of the separation of politics from sex fails to consider the representation of sex and its role in constructing the truth of sex today.

We must recognize that the pearl-clutching, anti–sex work moralists, who fear that porn is warping kids' minds, have a point. Online porn plays a powerful formative role in our lives, especially the millennials among us, informing notions of what sex *gets to be*. Given this fact, the need is obvious for political and ethical work toward a world of porn with better taxonomies and worker protections. My ex saw political heroes in his favorite porn stars—which would be fine, if he had thought of them first as workers. *There is no escaping economics.*

It's perhaps unsurprising, given the picture I've painted, that my relationship with this man ended in violent catastrophe. I grew to hate him for many reasons, but not before I had spent months, which bled into years, rethinking my approach to sexual desire. It was a revaluation of values and assumptions about what I want, for which I'll always be grateful, and in which I continue to engage to this day. In the years since we parted ways, I've had far more of the sex he would have deemed "radical" than I ever did with him. Some of it was transformative, some hot, some of it love, some boring and irritating—none of it revolutionary.

Technosociologist Zeynep Tufekci makes the point that traditional political movement tactics have gotten easier over the years, "partly thanks to technology": "A single Facebook post can help launch a large march! Online tools make it easier to coordinate phone calls, and even automate them. Legislators have figured this out; they are less likely to be spooked just by marches or phone calls (though those are good to do: their absence signals weakness)." Her point is that tactics that once signaled "underlying strength" no longer do, by virtue of the ease of reiterability; the threat is neutralized and the ruling order knows it. The same might be said of sexual practices that were once considered threats to capital's reproduction through the family form and property relations. Technocapital soothes the status quo: there can be polyamorous configurations with BDSM dungeons in the basement, but the houses are owned.

To be blunt: When there's a popular app for organizing your next queer orgy, how rupturous of our political status quo can the mere fact of such an orgy be? To be honest: that's not a totally rhetorical question.

Looking at Corpses

"Have you ever seen a white corpse in the news?" writer Ayesha Siddiqi asked on Twitter in 2015. "Seriously asking," she followed up, "have you ever seen news media circulate images of a white person's corpse?" Specifically, on the day Siddiqi asked, we did not. We did not see the bodies of two white journalists horrifically gunned down in Virginia by an ex-colleague on camera. Social media sites and major news outlets were swift to ban videos and images of their deaths.

I thought for some days on her question. I asked friends and colleagues. And while my rudimentary survey was by no means conclusive, it struck me that, no, I have not seen a white corpse in the news in recent memory. Not, perhaps, since twenty years ago, when an image of a firefighter carrying a dying little white girl from the rubble of the Oklahoma City bombing became iconic.

I have seen images of white people close to death, and they alone have caused controversy. There was much censure directed at the *New York Daily News* for publishing a front-page picture of Alison Parker, the anchor murdered on air, as she, still alive, looked into a firing gun. The *New York Post* was condemned for showing James Foley, also still alive, with the Islamic State executioner's knife pressed to his throat.

There are often ethical reasons that media producers, media sharers and media consumers urge these images be excised from our visual landscapes. News institutions instead publish images of vibrant white lives. Alison Parker smiling with her boyfriend; James Foley, flak-jacketed and vital, reporting in the field. Decency, privacy, respect, we are told—and that is well and good.

But we are often exposed to images of Black and brown corpses and deaths. Major news outlets released the CCTV footage of police gunning down twelve-year-old Tamir Rice in Cleveland. When Philando Castile was shot by a cop at point-blank range, while sitting in his car and obeying officers' orders, his traumatized girlfriend pulled out her smartphone and documented her partner bleeding out as the police continued to hold her at gunpoint. The footage was published by every major publication, viewer discretion advised. We saw, too, the corpses of dead Palestinian children struck by Israeli missiles on a Gazan beach in 2014; we have seen dozens of bodies pulled from the rubble of Assad regime air strikes. We didn't, for the most part, get their names.

Multiple news outlets published a most terrible image of a drowned Syrian toddler, Alan Kurdi (initially reported as Aylan Kurdi), one of twelve refugees who died, including his five-year-old brother, attempting to reach Greece. His tiny body washed up on a Turkish beach, waves lapped at his lifeless face. These images, originally captured by a Turkish news agency photographer, were featured on the front page of a number of major British newspapers, from tabloid to broadsheet.

And there are ethical grounds for the inclusion of such pictures in our visual fields. These images tell stories of racist, deadly police violence, colonial oppression and genocide. The week following the publication of the Alan Kurdi pictures, donations to the Swedish Red Cross campaign for Syrian refugees, for instance, was fifty-five times greater. (But within weeks, the amounts had dropped back down.) The then–prime minister, David Cameron, had described the refugees' coming to Europe as a "swarm" three months before Alan was found dead, one of 3,770 fatalities in the Mediterranean that year. One of the few to be *seen*.

I want to interrogate this double standard in visual media culture around racialized and marginalized deaths (and lives). What does it mean that when reporting on horrors perpetrated against certain persons we show death, and when others are the victims, we hide it?

If we do not see white corpses, it's because we don't need to. More precisely, the Western media and their interests don't need us, the audience and consumer, to do so. News of the brutal murder of a white individual—especially someone straight, white, professional and middle-class—doesn't need violent accompanying images to be registered by mainstream media as a violation, a brutality and (most importantly) a magnet for the eyeballs of their presumed readership or audience. As such, it is judged gratuitous and exploitative for publications to offer up a spectacle of white death. Family members and loved ones, too, have called for footage of corpses and executions to be removed from public media on the grounds that such imagery is dehumanizing. The memories of lived lives are reduced to corpses; and corpses in turn reduced to commodified spectacles. "That's not how life should be," wrote one of Foley's relatives, asking that the public not watch the journalist's beheading. And, certainly, that's not how life should be.

This tells us something about our current state of white supremacy, and who gets to be human(ized) in the first place. It is only by virtue of looking at the deaths, the corpses, and the soon-to-be corpses of Black people like Alton Sterling, Mike Brown, and Tamir Rice that the media even thought to ask about their lived lives at all and the structural plagues that cut them short. To be sure, were it not for the uprisings in Ferguson, Baltimore, Baton Rouge and beyond, demanding that Black Lives Matter, the media would have continued to look away.

It took nothing less than the brutal visual presentation of the Black dead, at the hands of US law enforcement, to gain white establishment recognition of the statement that "Black lives matter." It is as terrible as it is true: the consistent condition for a non-white life, particularly if it is poor and Black, to be humanized in the media is that it has been ended.

The media's double standards about showing corpses is a clear illustration of the brutal necropolitics to which so many Black, Muslim, indigenous, colonized and refugee lives are subjugated—that is, under the threat of, and in proximity to, death and disposal. As the first scholar to use the term, Achille Mbembe stressed that necropolitics does not reside only in the exercise of sovereignty via the power to kill, but the power to organize others' lives so that they are perpetually *exposed* to death, or experience a living death of slavery, imprisonment and segregation. In his 2003 article "Necropolitics," Mbembe names a number of techniques of necropower, such as "the selection of races, the prohibition of mixed marriages, forced sterilizations, even the forced sterilization of vanquished peoples." With many of their origins in colonial projects, these terror formations were reinscribed in the Nazi state, the plantation, the Palestinian occupation and apartheid, and continue to this day. Inextricable from racism but applied in the necropolitical subjugation of queer and trans communities, too, necropolitics enacts the "syntheses between massacre and bureaucracy, that incarnation of Western rationality."

Black male teens are twenty times more likely to be killed by police than their white peers in the US, a *ProPublica* investigation found. Poet Claudia Rankine examined the behaviors that have led to Black people being killed in recent years to produce a list of aligned prohibitions: "no hands in your pockets, no playing music, no sudden movements, no driving your car, no walking at night, no walking in the day, no turning onto this street, no entering this building, no standing your ground, no standing here, no standing there, no talking back, no playing with toy guns, no living while Black." It makes sense—awful sense—that life so organized by proximity to death, to execution, finds an appropriate visual expression in the media.

Judith Butler wrote in *Frames of War* (2016) that "we might think of war as dividing populations into those who are grievable and those who are not. An ungrievable life is one that cannot be mourned because it has never lived, that is, it has never counted as a life at all." This formulation does not suggest that an ungrievable life is grieved by no one, but rather that "war or, rather, the current wars, rely on and perpetuate a way of dividing lives into those that are worth defending, valuing, and grieving when they are lost, and those that are not quite lives, not quite valuable, recognizable or, indeed, mournable"—it asserts a grievable "we" and an un- or less grievable "them," whose existence and value is devalued when framed as a threat to ours.

Such was the violence in the media framing of the Iraq war and the entire demonizing War on Terror narrative that treats Muslims as only grievable if they are perceived as victims (of other Muslims) who could justify American military intervention, and ungrievable threats otherwise. We see divisions of grievability in Cameron's and many others' fearmongering over a refugee "swarm," an alleged threat to mythic "European values" (values that deserve, if they exist at all, to crumble if they entail such treatment of refugees); we see it in Trump's vicious immigration policies that would send refugees back to death and rape in Central America; we see it in every killing of a Black person legitimized by the stand-your-ground logics of racialized policing enshrined in US law. We see it enforced by the *New York Times* obituary that called Michael Brown "no angel," and when the only photos newspapers bother to find of murdered Black men are their mugshots.

In another important Twitter comment from Siddiqi on this issue, she asked, "When does documentation and archive continue dehumanization? When does bearing witness become spectacle?" She specifically highlighted how images of lynchings used to be sold as postcards. Documentation and archive, especially of corpses, always risks continued dehumanization. The desire that white lives be removed from such corporeal archiving highlights this point. Whether the publication and sharing of images of people's corpses intervenes with, upholds or simply reflects these necropolitical hierarchies of (un)grievability has no simple answer. It depends on who does the producing and sharing of such media, how it's done, and how we, as viewers, choose to respond.

There is a deplorable history of oppressive power structures using the spectacle of torturous killing to affirm their sovereign control, including the Islamic State's taped executions, public lynchings in the South, and all medieval public torture. Yet, as a mode of social control, such spectacles have not proven reliable. Foucault's *Discipline and Punish* opens with accounts of the gratuitous, public, hours-long torture and execution in France of Robert-François Damiens, a domestic servant who had attempted to assassinate King Louis XV. His flesh was torn away with hot pincers and molten lead poured on the wounds; his right hand was burned in sulfur, and after hours of attempting without success to tear him limb from limb with the power of six horses pulling him apart, the executioner hacked off his arms and legs with a knife. Foucault noted that "the few decades" that followed this, France's last drawing and quartering, "saw the disappearance of the tortured, dismembered, amputated body, symbolically branded on face or shoulder, exposed alive or dead to public view. The body as the major target of penal repression disappeared."

The punitive system's shift away from corporeal visibility to more "discretion in the art of inflicting pain" was not attributable, as Foucault noted, to some progressive idea of "humanization" alone, but rather to the state's concern that public executions were catalysts for civil disturbances and mass mobilizations, at the same time as an expansive administrative apparatus grew to make the act of punishment a sequestered affair. Behind the prison gates, the state could control a narrative of legitimized, procedural killing, foreclosing public pity and outrage on behalf of the ungrievable, unpitiable criminal other.

If there were no political potency in pathos, then Joseph Goebbels would not have written in 1941 against Jews who "send out their pitiable," as if their suffering were nothing but a ploy to manipulate those who witness it. It was a comment eerily echoed in the words of Israeli prime minister Benjamin Netanyahu when he said that Hamas was trying to garner international support by showing Gaza's "telegenically dead"—namely, some of the 448 children killed in nine months of Israeli attacks on occupied territory in 2014, according to the UN. Netanyahu's comment was an inadvertent admission that Israeli fire was producing the sort of dead bodies that make news—children are often telegenic.

There is a rich history of individuals and groups in righteous struggle choosing to make their beloved dead visible—a reflection, again, of a double standard, as so many white families urge that the bodies of their murdered loved ones remain out of public view. When Mamie Till insisted that the casket of her murdered, brutalized fourteen-year-old son, Emmett, be left open for public view in 1955, she said, "Let them see what I have seen." Emmett was lynched after being falsely accused of inappropriate flirting with a white woman; he was kidnapped and beaten to death by two brothers, who were then acquitted by an all-white jury. Tens of thousands of people visited his coffin, and the image of his mutilated, unrecognizable face was circulated in magazines and newspapers around the country. In the postcards of lynchings, which achieved small circulations in the South, the framing was often one of the public spectacle itself: large crowds around hardly visible, butchered, hanging bodies. Viewers are invited to see themselves in the vile mob. The photographs of Emmett Till, while dreadful, repeat no such violent spectacle. They are images of grief. In a picture published in *Jet* magazine, Mamie Till looks gently over her son's corpse; in another, taken at his funeral, she's bent double over his open casket, weeping and surrounded by embracing mourners. These images assert that Emmett Till was grieved, against a world that denied him a priori grievability in life.

It matters, when we question whether certain images of death serve to humanize or dehumanize the dead, that it was Mamie Till herself who declared, "Let them see." With this call she redrew the power structure of the "them" and the "we" who get to determine grievability. The same was not the case when the 2017 Whitney Biennial included a painting titled *Open Casket* by white artist Dana Shutz, which depicted, in impressionistic strokes, Emmett Till's casket surrounded by a blur of mourners. Once again, the pain of the Tills, Black pain, was conferred on an exploitable "them." An open letter by artist and writer Hannah Black, cosigned by dozens of artists, called for the painting to be removed and destroyed:

> That even the disfigured corpse of a child was not sufficient to move the white gaze from its habitual cold calculation is evident daily and in a myriad of ways, not least the fact that this painting exists at all. In brief: the painting should not be acceptable to anyone who cares or pretends to care about Black people because it is not acceptable for a white person to transmute Black suffering into profit and fun, though the practice has been normalized for a long time ... Through his mother's courage, Till was made available to Black people as an inspiration and warning. Non-Black people must accept that they will never embody and cannot understand this gesture: the evidence of their collective lack of understanding is that Black people go on dying at the hands of white supremacists.

It was a point well made, but lost on the commentators, and the Whitney, who jumped to the defense of Shutz (and white free speech). It should be well established by now that the mere reproduction of the spectacle of Black suffering does not challenge the system under which this suffering is normalized; cops with body-cams still kill Black people with impunity. Public outrage also followed (white) poet Kenneth Goldsmith's edited recital of Michael Brown's autopsy report and an art exhibit depicting Brown's corpse with a mannequin under a sheet in a Chicago gallery. Anger arose precisely because Brown's body, like Till's in Shutz's painting, was treated as a pure commodity alienated from Brown-the-person. The only thing perhaps more offensive than those artistic offerings is the truth they speak to—Brown's body was already a media spectacle and already dehumanized by white supremacy.

The difference between the artists' use of this horrible truth and the response of the Ferguson protesters and Black Lives Matter activists following Brown's death, or Mamie Till's act of resistance many decades before, was that the art doubled down on the spectacle-as-commodity. In contrast, the activism engaged in what NYU professor of media culture and communication Nicholas Mirzoeff calls "persistent looking," an act of defiance against historically racist technologies of visuality. Mirzoeff highlights, for example, the repetition of the chants "Hands Up, Don't Shoot!" and "I can't breathe!" as powerful repeat refusals to simply move beyond the deaths of Brown and Eric Garner. These protest rituals are calls to stay in the moment. "Die-in" demonstrations and the repetition of deceased people's names—tactics with their origins in AIDS crisis protest—similarly attempt to refuse that we move along. In *The Appearance of Black Lives Matter* (2017) Mirzoeff wrote of the "Hands Up, Don't Shoot!" chant and physical action:

It concentrates our attention on the vital moment (in the sense of living as well as essential) before the definitive violence. Those witnessing the action feel in that repeated present their choices for the future. The action prevents the media from its usual call for closure, healing, and moving on. Protesters choose to remain in that moment that is not singular, but has already been repeated. For Michael Brown, there was no choice. But when protesters reenact, they are making choices.

If Mirzoeff's appreciation of this chant seems overblown, it's worth recalling the speed with which the widely circulated, intolerable image of Alan Kurdi fell from the forefront of the public conscience and with it vanished the public's concern for refugees. In the first half of 2018, nearly three years after Alan's death, 1,130 people perished trying to cross the sea from North Africa to Europe. The ability of an image to produce outrage is one thing, to sustain it is another in a media environment in which 500 million tweets and 700 million Snapchats are posted every day. Turning affective outrage into effective resistance is a greater challenge still. Mirzoeff himself noted in a 2016 interview, "One can see that a single image, a single iteration, however powerful that image is, until it is taken up as part of a collective project, can't sustain the change we want to see longer than for a short period of time." As such, he highlights the strategic value of "persistent looking" evoked by direct actions in which activists place their bodies in spaces, streets and intersections, in which the demand is repeated, like Mamie Till's, to not look away.

Such direct action is not only an invocation of public grief for those who have been killed; it is an insistence on the presupposition that a life mattered and was grievable before it needed grieving.

13

Being Numerous

One photo from the sometime-halcyon days of Occupy Wall Street has come to haunt me. The image, which was used as the cover for the second issue of *Tidal*, Occupy's theory journal, at first glance seems to capture a trenchant insurrectionary tableau. A massive mob of protesters appears on the cusp of breaking down a fence, held up by a measly line of riot cops defending the emptiness of Duarte Square, a drab expanse of concrete in downtown Manhattan. Look closer, though, and a different scene comes into focus: no more than a scattered handful of protesters are actually pushing against the fence. The rest of the crowd, pressed tightly against each other, hold smartphones aloft, recording each other recording each other for the (assumed) viewers at home. The fence of Duarte Square was barely breached that December day in 2011.

Two years after that picture was taken, whistle-blower Edward Snowden's National Security Agency leaks asserted totalized surveillance as an undeniable fact of the American now. Years later still, it's hard to remember that it was ever a revelation that we are data bundles in government dragnets. That Occupy photo—in which a desire for insurrectionary action was paired with advanced technocapital's surveillance-control apparatus—telegraphed a fraught dynamic that in the years since has become impossible to ignore, but all too easy to forget.

The photo captured the near knee-jerk proclivity many participants in mass protests have developed to recount every action live over social media, with the idea that this was inherently bold and radical; taking the narrative of protest into our own hands, our own broadcast devices, refusing reliance on traditional media institutions. Regardless of where you stand on the question of whether social media platforms have helped, hindered, or otherwise shaped protest movements (or all of the above), the *Tidal* image took on a different valence in the years following the Snowden revelations. For the smartphones in that photograph were not only a hindrance to the crowd's purported effort to swarm Duarte Square; they were surveillance devices.

This much became undeniable by 2014 (at the latest): The devices and platforms we rely upon—to communicate, gather information and build solidarity—offer us up as ripe for constant surveillance. The surveillance state could not be upheld without its readily trackable denizens. To sidestep our tacit complicity in this would be to fail to recognize how deep our participation in our own surveillability runs—it's how we live.

Reflecting on that time, I can't remember what it was like for those thoughts to feel like something new and in need of saying. Surveillance is a condition of social life, given the ubiquity of social media; it seems almost quaint (and this is no good thing) that just a few years ago we were shocked to learn the extent of our mass surveillance state. This is, *of course*, how we live. But the NSA leaks were, at the time, a revelation. They shed light on a fearsome nexus between the government, communications and tech giants. And beyond this, they offered a lesson in the challenges of fighting a system of control in which we are complicit.

There was a certain folly, but also a commendable optimism, in the immediate, outraged responses to Snowden's leaks. Journalists and activists sought an object, a vessel, a villain. Who is to blame? Where are the bad guys? How do we fight back? There were obvious culprits in need of censure: whether it was then–director of national intelligence James Clapper, then–NSA director Keith Alexander, Google, AT&T, or the PRISM data collection and surveillance program, we looked to blame someone or something we could isolate and locate. Politicians' and activists' efforts centered on top-down NSA reform and demands for tech giants to be more transparent. As such, they missed the nuance and gravity of what was at stake.

It was a prime moment for bipartisan pantomime. Democrat and Republican lawmakers came together in performative outrage to demand an end to the NSA's bulk collection of Americans' communications data; signed into law in June 2015, the preposterously named USA Freedom Act gained traction primarily on this point. It proposed some limits on bulk data collection of Americans' communications, but it also restored some of the worst provisions of George W. Bush's 2001 Patriot Act. The Obama White House assembled advisory committees who duly issued lengthy reports and promised more reviews to come. Perhaps worst of all, scrambling for position as the "good guys," tech leviathans, including Google and Facebook, pushed publicly for greater transparency. It seems laughable now, after Facebook's opaque policies and products may have helped sway an election; nevertheless, every week brings a new promise of "transparency" from the great clouds of Silicon Valley.

The fight for bold executive and legislative reform of state surveillance came to little. For months during 2013 and 2014, we talked about the NSA. And then we didn't. Government agencies are still using programs like PRISM, launched in 2007, which authorizes the NSA to demand vast reserves of stored data, in concert with pretty much every major Silicon Valley company, including access to our private communications without warrants. None among the programs revealed in Snowden's trove, which incurred such public outrage at the time, has really stopped. The corporate-government surveillance nexus is going nowhere; the best these reform efforts had to offer is a surveillance state with mildly different contours.

By focusing on legible seats of power, activist groups and outraged political players largely sidestepped the question of how surveilled subjects uphold—cannot but uphold—their position as surveilled.

A lot of discussions about government surveillance were framed counterfactually: whether we *would* have consented to our current level of mass surveillance had we known what we were signing up for as digital denizens. In 2014, James Clapper admitted that the NSA should have been more open with the public about the ubiquitous hoarding of their communications. But, he doubled down: "If the program had been publicly introduced in the wake of the 9/11 attacks, most Americans would probably have supported it," he said. Clapper couldn't help but resort to a perverse conditional logic in which the public *would have* consented to what they *could not*, in fact, consent to. His post hoc assertion that the public would have agreed to mass government surveillance, had they been given advanced warning, is untestable—we can't go back to that moment. As Ben Wizner, legal adviser to Snowden and the director of the American Civil Liberties Union's Speech, Privacy and Technology Project, commented in response to Clapper, "Whether we would have consented to that at the time will never be known." We have not consented to our own constant surveillance, even if the way we live has produced it.

Since 2014, conversations about surveillance through techno-capitalism have shifted away from a focus on unconstitutional government spy programs, and toward questions about how, and to what corporate and political ends, tech giants extract and use our data. Or, more precisely, how these corporations use (and produce) us qua data; the data, after all, is not *ours*. This discursive shift makes sense; to focus primarily on the NSA incorrectly frames contemporary surveillance as a problem of unwanted, oppressive government scrutiny. This is, no doubt, a problem—as anyone summarily placed on a no-fly list would attest. But the government programs Snowden revealed operate over a terrain where mass (and mutual) surveillance is already the norm, the baseline, of social participation: the offering-up of ourselves, as surveillable subjects, through most every online interaction, all organized by a tiny number of vastly powerful corporations.

Writer and theorist Rob Horning summarized the problem well in a 2016 note published in the *New Inquiry*:

> Being watched qualifies us for the more specific forms of recognition that build our reputation and establish our economic viability. But the attention we experience as support and opportunity is also the data that sustains surveillance systems. We become complicit in surveillance's productivity, tracking ourselves and others, recognizing each other within spaces of capture. We want to be seen and want to control how we are seen, but we accept that one can come only at the expense of the other.

The extent to which we truly "want" and "accept" these conditions is moot. While we are unquestionably active participants in upholding a state of surveillance, to suggest that we are therefore consenting would be to overstate our choice in the matter. We are not all inherently reliant, as a point of economic necessity, on surveillance-enabling devices and interfaces (although many workers, like Uber drivers and TaskRabbit cleaners are). However, participation in surveillance systems is inescapable for those who abide by the social and economic spirit of the now, because these Silicon Valley–owned networks and interfaces have become the stage on which the social, the intimate and the commercial—even the political and the revolutionary—are enacted.

Paul Virilio, one of the most prescient thinkers of how technology (re)orders the world, talked about accidents. Each technology, from the moment of its invention, carries its own accident (its potential for accident)—it introduces a type of accident, a scale of disaster, into the world that had not existed before. The invention of a technology contains the invention of that technology's severest accident, as well as its minor potential downsides and failings. As Virilio put it, "When you invent the ship, you also invent the shipwreck; when you invent the plane you also invent the plane crash; and when you invent electricity, you invent electrocution ... Every technology carries its own negativity, which is invented at the same time as technical progress." The fact that we presume innovative advancement without damage is hubris worthy of Icarus. As Virilio saw it, technology containing its own accident is "so obvious that being obliged to repeat it shows the extent to which we are alienated by the propaganda of progress."

Virilio's framework rejects a dim binary in which we must deem our current and developing technologies "good" or "bad." Rather, it demands a constant ethical calculus: we must ask of a technological possibility what potential accidents it contains, and whether they are tolerable. It's not always knowable, but it is always askable. And better asked sooner, rather than later. As Virilio pointed out in 1995, high-speed trains were made possible because older rail technologies had produced a form of traffic control that allowed trains to go faster and faster without risking disastrous collisions. The accident had been considered. But, "there is no traffic control system for today's information technology," he wrote then, and again, more recently: "We still don't know what a virtual accident looks like." But he knew this accident would be "integral and globally constituted"; such is the totality of online networks' enmeshment with everyday life, all at instantaneous speed. "We are pressed, pressed on each other / We will be told at once / Of anything that happens"—so the poet George Oppen foresaw in his great 1968 work *Of Being Numerous*.

For its developers, advertisers and the government, surveillance is not an accident of social media. For many users—those seeking only a network of communication and recognition, plus a few well-targeted ads—surveillance here is a most tolerable accident of networked technologies. However, for some of us (and it should be more of us—I know I should feel this way more often, when instead I click on the recommended ad), it is an *intolerable* accident that we wish we could have foreseen. When I joined Facebook as an undergraduate student in order to keep in touch with school friends, I didn't even think about it. And here, again, consent is moot: there is a small, elite regime of expertise when it comes to the techno-scientific knowledge necessary to analyze, before too late, the accident toward which we, as users, are hurtling. But of the Silicon Valley scions, it is fair to say: you knew, or should have known.

Enough guilt-ridden former Facebook and Apple programmers have come forward with tepid mea culpas about designing features aimed at triggering addictive behaviors and user reliance. Like a casino manager admitting that they keep out natural light and serve free coffee all night for a reason. And, as Horning also noted, there is a pleasure in giving over to algorithmically organized experiences, through feeds and curated ads and suggestions, which cater to and deliberate (for us) our desires: "Such platforms teach users helplessness. Staging information overload deliberately helps with the lessons. The point is to make the surrender pleasurable."

Our engagement with the devices of the surveillance state goes deeper than the technological tools we use—indeed these are not simply tools, but apparatuses. In "What Is an Apparatus?," Italian philosopher Giorgio Agamben argues that "ever since *Homo sapiens* first appeared, there have been apparatuses, but we could say that today there is not even a single instant in which the life of individuals is not modeled, contaminated, or controlled by some apparatus." For Agamben, an apparatus is not simply a technological device, but "literally anything that has in some way the capacity to capture, orient, determine, intercept, model, control, or secure the gestures, behaviors, opinions, or discourses of living beings." As such, a language is an apparatus as much as an iPhone. He wrote of his "implacable hatred" for cell phones and his desire to destroy them all and punish their users. But then he noted that this is not the right solution.

The "apparatus" cannot simply be isolated in the device or the interface—say, the smartphone or the website—because apparatuses are shaped by, and shape, the subjects that use them. Destroying the apparatus would entail destroying, in some ways, the subjects who create and are in turn created by it. There's no denying that the apparatuses by which we have become surveillable subjects are also systems through which we have become our current selves, tout court, through social media and trackable online communication—working, dating, shopping, networking, archived, ephemeral and legible selves and (crucially) communities. A mass Luddite movement to smash all smartphones, laptops, GPS devices, and so on would ignore the fact that it is no mere accident of history that millions of us have chosen, albeit via an overdetermined "choice," to live with and through these devices.

"The California Ideology"—the dream (dreamt by a handful of rich, white men in the early 1990s) that the internet would be a democratizing force of decentralized power and knowledge—was always a myth born of myopic thinking, one which failed to take into account that the internet was born within, not beyond, the strictures of capitalist relationality and brutal social hierarchy. Public access to information expanded on a vast scale, but at the same time, consolidation of power over the information *network* was stunning. As writer and neuroscientist Aaron Bornstein has pointed out,

Each year more data is being produced—and, with cheap storage and a culture of collection, preserved—than existed in all of human history before the internet. It is thus literally true that more of humanity's records are held by fewer people than ever before, each of whom can be—and, we now know, are—compelled to deliver those records to the state.

When in 2009, then-executive chairman of Google Eric Schmidt said that "if you have something that you don't want anyone to know, maybe you shouldn't be doing it in the first place," he exemplified the sort of Silicon Valley privilege that undergirds unfettered surveillance systems. This dangerous Google ethic forgets that not every individual is afforded the opportunity to make the details of their life, personal records, preferences, and histories available for public consumption without consequence. A highly paid Silicon Valley engineer may freely Instagram his deviance at Burning Man with abandon. But undocumented immigrants, sex workers, and incarcerated individuals—to name just a few marginalized communities —don't necessarily have that privilege. Beyond this, resistance to mass surveillance is not only an issue of what we may or may not want to hide, but how our lives are organized and susceptible to social control, how we become, as Foucault put it, "docile bodies."

For the most part, resistance to surveillance is framed in terms of privacy—be it insisting on better privacy policies from tech companies and the state, or encouraging better privacy practices among individuals. Such efforts may take the form of resistance through transparency: What is being done with our data? What do companies know about us? Or otherwise, that of protection through obfuscation: encryption services, Onion routing, surveillance-thwarting makeup. The options are reformist and reactive, at best. Interferences, hacks and ruptures in networks-as-normal, when carried out by nongovernmental actors, tend to be fleeting. Such is the asymmetry of power. Save for a Luddite revolution, an option available and desirable to very few, our current, collective options for resistance illustrate the extent to which surveillance technologies are sewn into—and give shape to—the fabric of daily life. To partake in the benefits, pleasures, necessities and inescapabilities of social media participation, surveillance is a "form of life" in the sense that Wittgenstein used the term: surveillability is the background context by which these interactions and experiences are made possible. Surveillance is not epiphenomenal to social media life—it is its bedrock. Under late capitalism, that is.

This is what Oppen anticipated: "Obsessed, bewildered / By the shipwreck / Of the singular / We have chosen the meaning / Of Being Numerous." He was not, half a century ago, hinting at totalized surveillance through social media, but he speaks to the interrelations undergirding our current condition. We participate in the social order; we avoid the "shipwreck" of our singular selves, with which we are nonetheless obsessed, but we have not yet (for now) chosen to be collective, or communized or united. We have chosen to be numerous: as online selves, we are enumerated as surveilled data points. We live by and through the numbers: the likes, the clicks, the follows. Crucially, though, Oppen wrote that it was "the meaning" of being numerous that we have chosen; and there is hope in the thought that we might choose differently, together, this *meaning*.

Through enmeshed digital and meatspace lives, millions of people have, at times, already chosen to be numerous in ways never before possible. Engagement on social media produces and demands complicated sets of relations, connections, truths and illusions. And it has at times been fueled by, and in turn produced, revolutionary subjects. There is no question, for example, that Twitter shed a novel light on Iran's 2009 Green Revolution, on the Tunisian revolution of 2010 to 2011, and

Egypt's 2011 revolution. Social media were both a product of, and a factor in, creating the conditions of possibility for these uprisings. Tweets shaped their narratives because tweets *were* their narrative. Tweets called bodies into insurrectionary spaces, and bodies used Twitter to expand those spaces further. Most every street protest I've attended for the last seven or so years has been to some extent organized through social media. The #MeToo hashtag fostered important discussions and connections over the ubiquity of patriarchy and sexual violence, while helping fuel concrete collective action taken by hotel and fast-food workers. Hashtags as social movement tools have profound limitations (suffice it to mention #Kony2012); but so do all tactics. Critique of so-called "slacktivism" is beyond the purview of these paragraphs. My point here is simply that there are notable ways in which our being numerous online has augmented our power to effect social change.

That does not mean we can talk of "Twitter revolutions," as the media once reductively and absurdly buzzed about the Arab Spring; but social media's usefulness in revolutionary struggle and protest (and they have been useful) further complicates the question of whether we can tolerate the "accident"—by our lights, in Virilian terms—of surveillance. Not to mention the "accident" that these platforms offer equal opportunity (with scant interest in oversight) for fascists to become numerous beyond a given locality, too.

Can we tolerate that our digital habits and reliances contain accidents for us, which are desired outcomes for those who control the digital infrastructure? In a 2000 interview, Virilio said, "Resistance is always possible" and called first of all for the development of "a democratic technological culture." As he put it: "Technoscientific intelligence is presently insufficiently spread among society at large to enable us to interpret the sorts of technoscientific advances that are taking shape today." He was right, but the answer is not that we all learn how to code and hack (although that wouldn't hurt). The problem is that now the technoscientific power over the infrastructure of our social media lives is even more consolidated and hierarchical than is corporate and governmental control over the infrastructure of the streets in a city.

It's hard to see a way out of the dilemma. But this is not to say would-be resisters aren't trying.

Cultural critic Ben Tarnoff, for example, has put forward the idea of socializing our data, under the template of democratic resource nationalism, as a way to cede power (and the extractive value captured from the data we produce) from the tech giants back to the denizens of the digital commons. As he explained it in the journal *Logic*:

> Such a move wouldn't necessarily require seizing the extractive apparatus itself. You don't have to nationalize the data centers to nationalize the data. Companies could continue to extract and refine data—under democratically determined rules—but with the crucial distinction that they are doing so on our behalf, and for our benefit … In exchange for permission to extract and refine our data, companies would be required to pay a certain percentage of their data revenue into a sovereign wealth fund, either in cash or stock.

If the data were not privately owned—if we could truly democratically determine the rules that govern how companies extract it and for what—the social media sites of extraction would look very different. We can't talk of a "democratic technological culture" while Big Data remains undemocratized; and regulation alone won't get us there. Tarnoff recognizes that democratization requires that data be used to benefit the public *directly*, rather than through the false promises of the corporations who currently benefit from a regime of capture and exploitation; his plan would use democratic control of data, on which late capitalism runs, to undermine capitalism. Marx would be thrilled.

Tarnoff stressed the difficulty and risks involved in such a reconfiguration of data: "Transparency, coordination, automation—if these have democratic possibilities, they have authoritarian ones as well." Such a thought is, in itself, what it looks like to consider aloud the ethics of a possible technological future and the accidents it contains. I'm not suggesting that the nationalization of data is the one correct solution, or even a possible one; it is, as Tarnoff notes, "delightfully utopian." But it is, at the very least, a vista to a "democratic technological culture"—one to which we might be able to consent, in great numbers.

Of Suicide

Some suicides are akin to manslaughter. I don't mean that they are criminal. I mean simply that some suicide belongs in that liminal category between the accidental and the intentional. An attempt is made on a life without premeditation—messy and unmeticulous. It is impossible to answer definitively, "Did they mean to do it?"

These are those anguished leaps for oblivion, which—not for want of medical and psychiatric pathology—remain mysterious. These acts stand in stark contrast to the deliberated acts of suicide, either assisted or solo, in which an individual determines that their life is better ended. When twenty-nine-year-old Brittany Maynard, facing swift and terminal brain degeneration from cancer, moved to Oregon—where it is legal to die with a physician-prescribed lethal dose of barbiturates—she asserted sovereignty over her own life. The young woman took to YouTube before her scheduled November death to publicize her case and argue that others, like her, should be permitted to "die with dignity." Cases need not be as clean cut or imminently terminal as Maynard's to be defensible. I see no moral ill in deciding to die; players should be able to fairly choose how many hours to strut and fret upon this stage.

Had any of my attempted suicides been successful, I believe they would have been equally morally defensible. But it would not have been death with dignity, nor with deliberation. "Crime of Passion, Your Honor," I'd tell the judge, "it was manslaughter."

I've tried to kill myself twice. I feel a twinge of disingenuousness even writing that, because those are uncompromising words, "I tried to kill myself." The sentence sits ill with me, though it is straightforwardly verifiable: twice I have landed in a Brooklyn emergency room because I overdosed. Most recently it was fistfuls of ibuprofen and Seroquel—an antipsychotic medication, prescribed for bipolar disorder. (This gives some context, I suppose.) Just over a year before that, it was anything I could find in the disheveled bedroom I shared with the violent and broken man with whom I had planned to spend my life (there's some more context for you)—painkillers, antidepressants, Klonopin, some methadone a passing junkie had left behind.

All of which is to say, these were the sorts of concerted efforts that left me hooked up to IV fluids, Under Observation and shitting black activated charcoal for a week. And that gets called attempted suicide. In both instances, though, intent was a gray area. Distressed, unplanned, and, thankfully, unsuccessful, these were attempts at self-annihilation rooted in a transient despair. My overdoses are memory black spots. I don't remember the ambulance or how my best friend knew to get there or when they swapped my clothes for the green gown that would make even a paragon of wellness appear sickly. I don't remember deciding to take the pills or deciding that I wish I hadn't. I do remember the way a handful of ibuprofen felt in my palms, sweaty and melting red dye, though not in my mouth nor going down my throat. I do remember that I couldn't form words when asked, "Did you intend to kill yourself?" or "What happened?" I was too out of it to speak and, in truth, I didn't know. I still don't.

I both did and did not intend to die. EMTs and ER staff, however, don't barter in such equivocations. Risk assessments have to be made, and patients must be sorted into the suicidal and the accidental. Psychiatry distinguishes between suicidal ideation, intent and risk. Ideation is common and, while a mark of certain depressions, is no consistent indication of intent or risk to self-harm or death. I've thought about the fact of suicide for as long as I can remember—but those familiar vertiginous fancies, arising, say, at the edge of a subway platform ("how strange, just one more step, such a small and common act, most simple, most difficult")—are a world away from the implacable terror or dread-like sensation that preceded my suicidal acts. Though still overly simplistic, the differentiation between suicidal ideation, intent and material risk goes some way to acknowledge that our sovereign relations with our own mortality, our control over it, are fraught and complicated.

It is correct and unavoidable to point, in cases like mine, to mental illness and substance abuse, wherein the two meet. It is also irredeemably circular. Unpremeditated suicide, manslaughter suicide, is understood as the act of an unsound mind. Pathology, bartering as it does in cause and effect, posits such suicide as an effect of mental illness and seeks causal explanation in the realm of mental illness. In his 2010 book *Suicide: Foucault, History and Truth*, sociologist Ian Marsh notes that suicide is "unequivocally" treated as "an issue to be categorized, managed, controlled and prevented, and solutions to the problem are pharmacological and psychotherapeutic." As Marsh argues, psychiatry has constructed a "regime of truth" that produces a "compulsory ontology of pathology in relation to suicide"; we can't even think about impulsive suicidal acts without reference to mental illness. Like any regime of truth, suicide-as-pathology posits a particular world of subjects, objects and relations in order to make sense of suicide. Above all, it assumes that sense can be made.

But the pathologized suicidal subject is ontologically weird. "She killed herself"—the sentence's subject and object are the same individual. It is no stranger than any other instance of apparent subject/object collapse—a perennial problem philosophy finds for itself. In Enlightenment empiricist thinker

David Hume's troubled appendix to his *Treatise on Human Nature*, published in 1738, he expresses some despair that the self presents as no more than a contiguous series of mental states; but, this being so, the pesky "I" that experiences these states persists, evading reduction to empirical explanation. "When I turn my reflection on myself," wrote Hume, "I never can perceive this self without some one or more perceptions; nor can I ever perceive any thing but the perceptions." The self as object, this set of perceptions, cannot account for the phenomenon of the self as subject. Of this quandary, the Scottish philosopher wrote, "I find myself involved in such a labyrinth, that, I must confess, I neither know how to correct my former opinions, nor how to render them consistent."

I find myself, the suicidal subject, irretrievably tangled in this dualism of self: both attempted killer and her would-be victim. I designate the former as unwell and monstrous, an Edward Hyde of my own making, my own being. Petrified that she might strike again, I try to obliterate her, first with medication, more sleep, and appointments in a psychiatrist's office twelve floors above Union Square. The view from the window captures every Manhattan skyline landmark, like a snow globe. Philosophically, my split suicidal self is incoherent; therapeutically, the split provides some relief and refuge from the nagging question of whether I did or did not really mean to die. Placing the suicidal subject within the realm of the clinically pathological provides a story that makes sense of my attempted self-manslaughter. Yet, for reasons unclear and probably historical, the problem of intent lingers. It's not a question I seek out, but one that haunts me: Did I mean to do it?

The need (or the feeling of need) for answers about intent emerges in part from the gravity of the matter at hand. When Hume, one of the key defenders of suicide in the Western philosophical canon, wrote in 1750, "I believe that no man ever threw away life while it was worth keeping. For such is our natural horror of death that small motives will never be able to reconcile us to it," he gestured to the weightiness normally, or normatively, applied to considerations of mortality. If all suicides were of the deliberate and considered variety, like Brittany Maynard's, Hume would have been quite right. His proposition that an individual is a correct judge of when to end her own life posits the suicidal subject as an ultimately rational actor.

Hume's 1755 tract, "Of Suicide," is an attempt to salvage suicide as defensible within a context that demanded that for an act to be considered moral, it must abrogate duty to neither God nor the Laws of Nature. I am unburdened by religiosity, and, without a metaphysical commitment to life's inherent value, I'm not interested in a moral argument in defense of suicide. I simply suggest, contra Hume, that not all suicides or attempted suicides involve a suicidal subject reconciling herself with the "natural horror of death." In my case, at least, the brute fact of having tried to die—and there is horror in that—only hit post hoc and remains unreconciled.

Any survey of suicidal intent is stymied by survivor bias; even the most diligent research can't reach beyond the grave and ask those who take their own lives whether they had really "meant" to. Some leave notes, some don't. But we must avoid the sort of tautological thinking that asserts that if a suicide attempt was successful, then the actor had really intended to succeed in ending their lives. Even with a complete and coherent pathological explanation of a suicide attempt, intent can remain a gray area.

Attempts to attribute intent, or complete lack thereof, in suicide cases are understandable. Intent is dramatized in suicide narratives because the stakes are so very high. Grasping for understanding, we run the risk of ascribing complete and reasonable deliberation (such as in Maynard's case), or a psychopathology in which any sort of intention is impossible. Suicide becomes the purview of either the mad or the meaningful, and nothing in between. Speaking from little more than personal experience, I suggest that it might not be so. Despite all the answers psychiatry and pharmacology have to offer, none of them can resolve the haunting self-knowledge that in some sense, I tried to die, both meaningfully and without really meaning it. An explanation within the discourse of mental illness feels necessary, but insufficient. And I tentatively conclude that this is okay. While impulsive self-manslaughter attempts can be explained, the feeling of having committed the act will persist like a haunting and threat, unsettling and unsettled. Maybe I just haven't come to terms with it yet, but something tells me the terms might simply not be there. Like Hume, I find myself involved in the labyrinth of trying to locate an "I," which maybe I cannot.

Meanwhile, life continues. In the weeks following my last overdose, my days were surprisingly normal. I had scared myself, and I renewed commitments to better self-care; I did that the previous time, too. Surviving my own attempted manslaughter brought no revelation. On a few fleeting instances I have paused for something like sentimentality, or appreciation. My best friend was sick one night. I sat with her, stroked her hair and watched her fall asleep; I was pleased to watch her feel better, and was pleased to be alive to watch her feel better. My lover's body was always warm, remarkably warm. He felt like energy, and once or twice in the weeks after I didn't die, I pressed my face against his chest to appreciate heat and heartbeat. After writing that sentence, I rested two fingers against my throat to feel my own pulse.